● Halifax

HUSETTS

Atlantic Ocean

T

S

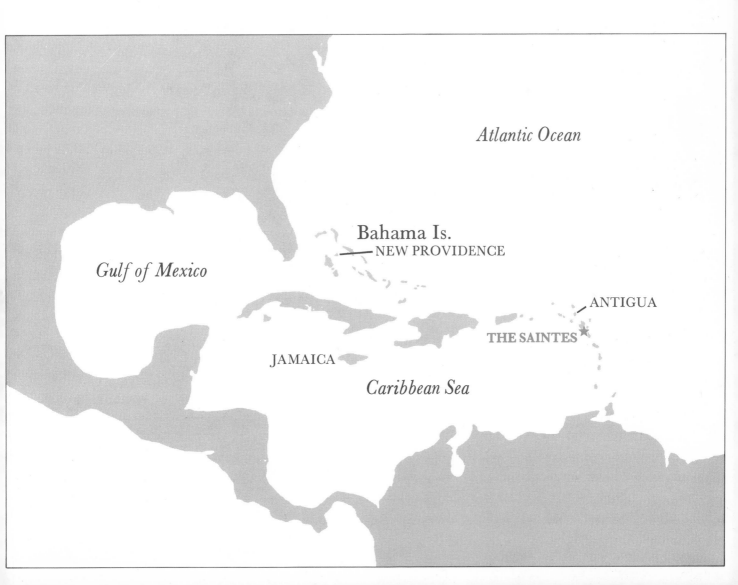

Atlantic Ocean

Gulf of Mexico

Bahama Is.
—— NEW PROVIDENCE

—— ANTIGUA

THE SAINTES ★

JAMAICA

Caribbean Sea

Armies of the American Revolution

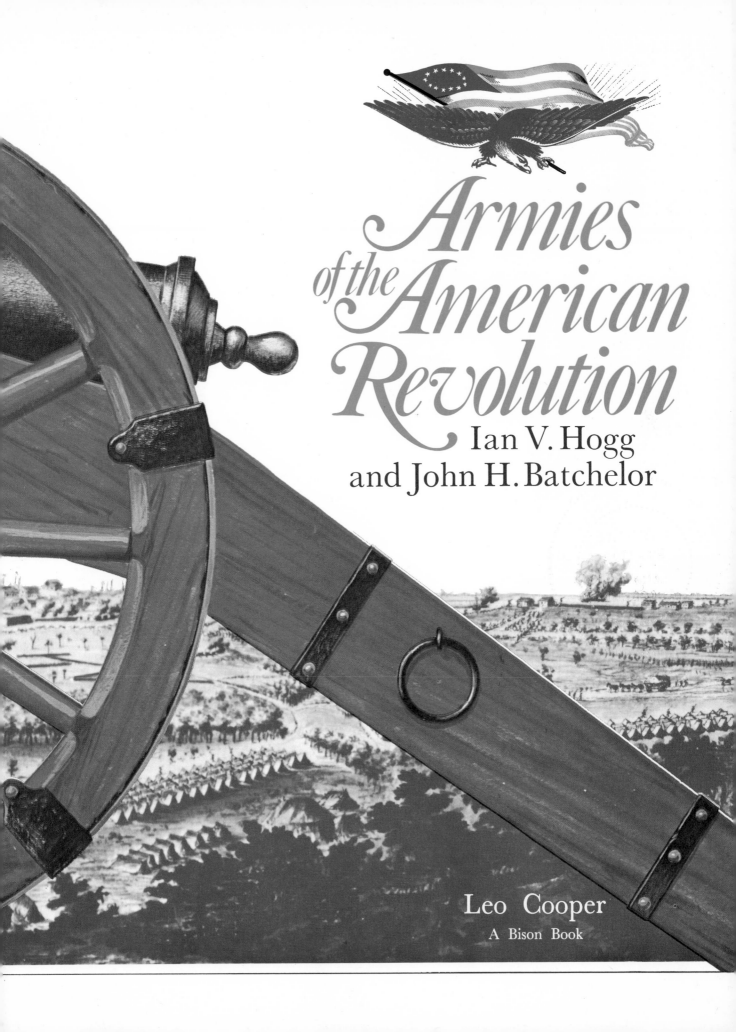

Armies of the American Revolution

Ian V. Hogg
and John H. Batchelor

Leo Cooper

A Bison Book

Armies of the American Revolution
by Ian Hogg and John Batchelor

Published for Bison Books Ltd. by
Leo Cooper Ltd., 196 Shaftesbury Avenue,
London WC2

Printed and bound in Great Britain by
Morrison & Gibb Ltd, London and Edinburgh

ISBN 0 85052 190 4

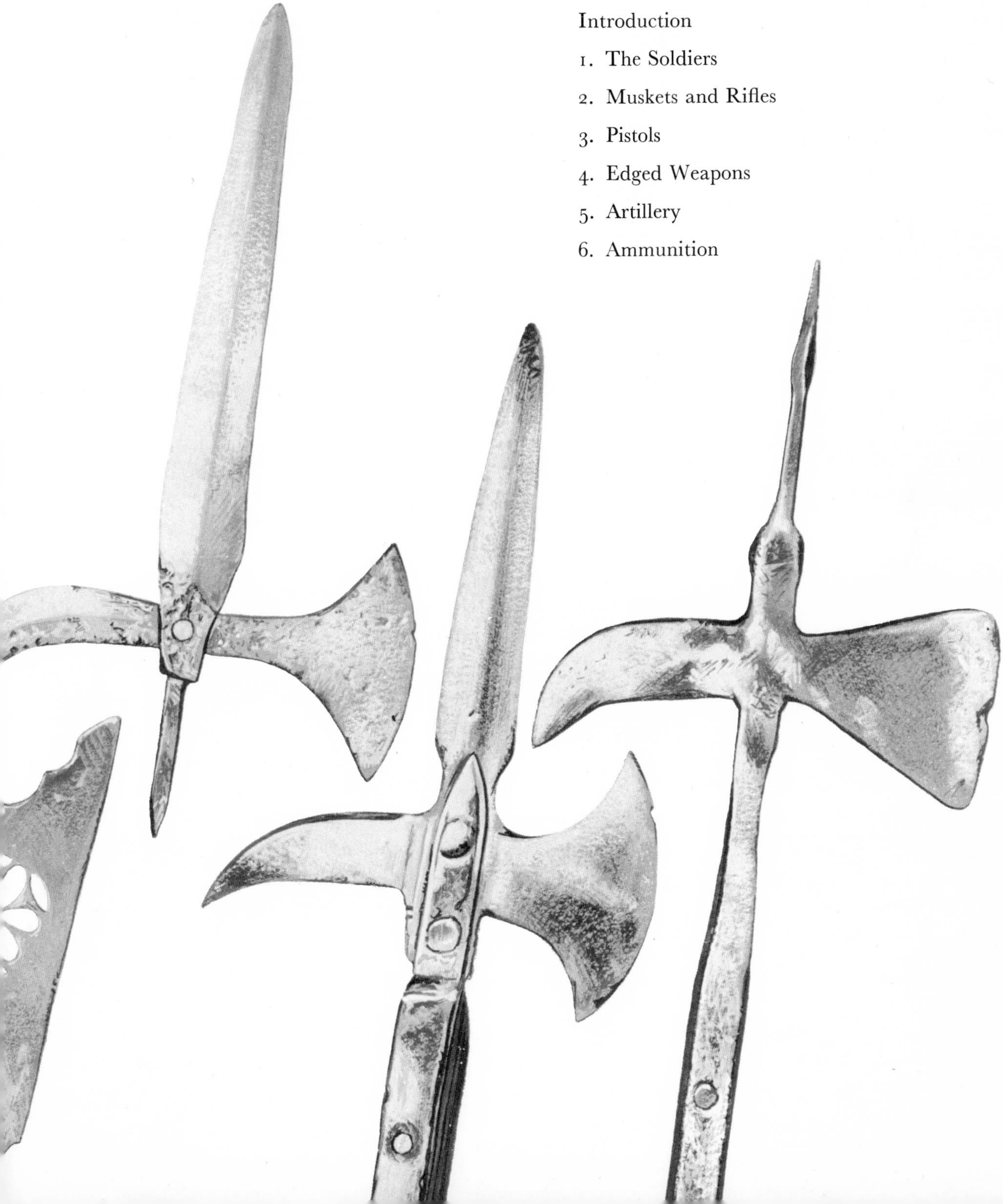

Introduction

There have been at least nine world wars in modern times, starting with the War of the League of Augsburg——essentially a European conflict which spread to the Americas——and continuing through the many dynastic wars of the 18th century. One world war, the French and Indian War, started in North America and spread to Europe to become the Seven Years War, in which Frederick the Great found himself surrounded by enemies and beleaguered in Berlin, while the British seized Canada, French ports in India, Cuba and the Philippines (until the diplomats finally sorted things out at the conference table). The wars of the French Revolution, which were continued by Napoleon, were likewise fought on many continents, the American War of 1812 being one of them. And, of course, the world wars of the 20th century are all too familiar. But only one of these nine world wars began as a colonial civil war and spread throughout the world to engulf virtually every important naval and land power and a number of less important ones. This was the War of the American Revolution.

Britain had governed her thirteen colonies very loosely since the first Virginians had settled Jamestown at the beginning of the 17th century. The colonists had gained a number of political rights

Above: Original French battle map of Yorktown, the American victory which decided the war.
Below: The generals who won at Yorktown. Washington is the second from the left.

which they never possessed in England. The ownership of land on a continent almost bereft of people (scarcely a million Indians of various tribes were scattered unevenly between northern Canada and the Rio Grande) was considerably easier than in Britain, where the enclosures movement was driving many farmers into urban centres or abroad. But after the French and Indian War, which gave Britain control of the whole of North America, regulations which had long been ignored began to be enforced. New and more stringent measures to get the Americans to pay taxes to the Crown were invoked. Intransigence on the part of George III and his Prime Minister, Lord North, was met with equal stubbornness on the part of patriots like Samuel Adams and Patrick Henry, who pressed for American representation in Parliament at Westminster. Many Americans wanted their rights as Englishmen which the Crown denied them, but many others were quite satisfied to have things continue as before. It is often forgotten that something like one-third of the British subjects in the American colonies were loyal to King and Empire throughout the Revolutionary War. Probably another third shifted loyalties according to the direction of the political wind and their own self-interest. It was by no means unanimously agreed that a revolution should take place in 1776 or any other time. The colonists were bitterly divided, and the 'shot heard round the world' fired at Lexington in effect began a civil war within the American colonies which the British authorities thought they could suppress without great difficulty.

The early stages of the Revolutionary War only slightly weakened British determination to suppress the rebels. True, the defense of Bunker Hill convinced the British that those Americans who were willing to fight had a determination to persevere, and the American invasion of Canada in the winter of 1775–76 showed the British that the armies of Benedict Arnold and Richard Montgomery were daring and resourceful. But the invasion of Canada ultimately proved a failure; Montgomery was killed and Arnold later became a traitor to the cause for which he once fought. George Washington, Commander-in-Chief of the Continental Armies, was soon faced with a seemingly insurmountable dilemma. Wars are won by victories on the field, not by scaling oratorical heights, and his armies were losing. Pushed back from Brooklyn Heights, forced to leave New York to the enemy, defeated at White Plains later in 1776, Washington retired to his winter quarters at Morristown, New Jersey, facing a collapse of morale and impending military defeat.

The Americans were short of supplies of every type. Although their marksmen were excellent, weapons were in short supply and money was needed to finance the military effort. Continental currency was prized far less than British gold sovereigns by provisioners in America, and American paper money was soon to be devalued to something like 2% of its face value. The troops of Gentleman Johnny Burgoyne, on the other hand, were well supplied and paid in coin of the realm. While Benjamin Franklin vainly tried to convince France that she should support the new Republic, the British Army leisurely prepared to cut New England off from the rest of the country by a two-pronged invasion of the Hudson Valley. The United States desperately needed a victory to convince France that she was worthy of her support.

That victory came at Saratoga in the autumn of 1777. Burgoyne, surrounded by his mistresses and ample quantities of champagne, found the forests of New York State less comfortable when his forces were surrounded and obliged to capitulate. Even though the Americans were too weak to exploit the Saratoga victory, it was unquestionably one of the two most important battles of the war. The British now virtually gave up all hope of conquering the North, and from then on they concentrated their military activities in the South. From this point on, naval blockade, coastal raids, and retention of most of the main cities would be the British strategy. But for the Americans, Saratoga was vital because Franklin in Paris was able to convince French Foreign

Minister Vergennes that backing the United States was a sound proposition after all.

In February 1778 France recognized the United States and promised her military and financial assistance, as well as a guarantee that no separate peace would be made with Britain. Spain joined her Bourbon ally the following year, and by 1781 most of Europe, including Holland's important fleet, was either on the side of the United States or benevolently neutral towards the anti-British cause. Holland and Spain harassed British shipping in East Indian waters, the Mediterranean and the Caribbean, while France attempted to regain much of the colonial territory seized from her at the end of the Seven Years War. Britain was cut off from most of her naval stores, and the War of American Revolution had become a new world war.

French aid took many forms. Loans were given to prop up the sinking Continental currency. This was vital, as Congress was obliged to stop its issuance in 1779, causing a revolt among some Connecticut, New Jersey and Pennsylvania troops. The receipt of over four million dollars' worth of French loans helped to solve the immediate financial crisis. The arrival of French arms, some French troops, and key French generals also made a vast difference.

So did the French Navy. The arrival of Admiral d'Estaing off New York threatened British supply lines for a time, and General Rochambeau was able to land his troops in Rhode Island in 1780 without opposition. The arrival of the French volunteer aristocrat, the 24-year-old Marquis de Lafayette, gave Washington a trusted subordinate whose enthusiasm was matched by considerable expertise. The addition of the Germans, von Steuben and de Kalb, and the Poles, Kosciusko and Pulaski, added further quality to American generalship. Indeed, without all this foreign aid the American cause would have been hopelessly lost after Washington's disastrous winter of 1777–78 at Valley Forge.

But even with external assistance the war was not going well for the Americans. Despite the fact that George Rogers Clark was seizing the British forts of Kaskaskia and Vincennes in the Middle West in 1779, the British held their most important strong points, like Detroit and Michilimackinac, throughout the war. Guerrilla fighters like Francis Marion, the 'Swamp Fox', harassed the British in the South, but in the main, the British conducted their Southern campaign rather successfully. Savannah was easily captured, and the most important port in the South, Charleston, was taken by the British, along with over 5000 American soldiers under the command of General Benjamin Lincoln. As Lord Charles Cornwallis marched north through the Carolinas, Horatio Gates, the hero of Saratoga, was sent to stop him. At Camden, South Carolina, Gates suffered a shattering defeat in August 1780. Although a unit of a thousand Redcoats was killed or captured in October at Kings Mountain, British losses were generally sporadic and did not prevent their drive northward.

Eventually Nathaniel Greene, Gates' replacement, aided by Daniel Morgan, blunted the British drive to the north at Cowpens, near Kings Mountain. Although the British won a series of minor technical victories in the Carolinas, Cornwallis cautiously decided to move into Virginia where the interior was less hostile than in the Carolinas. By 1781 effective British power in the South was confined to the ports of Charleston and Savannah and to those areas in Virginia which were controlled by Benedict Arnold, now in the service of the Crown. Cornwallis' arrival in Virginia boosted the British forces there to over 7000, and Cornwallis began to build a fortified base at Yorktown for his Virginia campaign.

Washington recognized an opportunity to break the British will to continue the war when Cornwallis effectively pinned himself down at Yorktown. Although Lafayette's forces in Virginia were unequal to the task of defeating Cornwallis, with the help of the French Navy, the Franco-American forces could be augmented and Cornwallis surrounded. Admiral de Grasse had arrived off the Virginia coast with some 28 ships, which blocked the escape route of the

British. He landed about 3000 French soldiers to help Lafayette prevent Cornwallis' escape, and in a naval battle off the Virginia coast in September 1781, British Admirals Graves and Hood were badly outnumbered and defeated by de Grasse. At this stage Washington and Rochambeau, taking most of their forces from the New York area, joined Lafayette to close in for the kill.

The siege of Yorktown ensued, with Cornwallis outnumbered by better than two to one. His entire army was forced to surrender on 18 October 1781, and in the words of Lord North, 'it was all over'. Despite the fact that Britain was, even in defeat, the greatest power in the world, she had been beaten by a badly equipped, poorly supplied, often badly generaled colonial army, assisted by a number of important European powers. This defeat, which put an end to the First British Empire and gave birth to the American Republic, destroyed Britain's willingness to continue the fight.

The British Army, which had distinguished itself so brilliantly at Quebec only a generation before, and which was to conduct itself with honor in the Peninsular campaign and at Waterloo a generation hence, had somehow been outmatched. How was this possible? Certainly Washington and his generals mastered tactics during the war; Washington's use of artillery at Dorchester Heights and Gates' use of artillery at Saratoga indicated that. But the British forces were better-trained, better-equipped and more experienced. Was this an example of a volunteer army fighting for a cause in which they believed and winning because they opposed a largely mercenary force which fought for personal gain or money? Was this a victory won by superiority of weapons? Was the war won by logistics or psychology or foreign aid or plain luck?

There is, of course, no simple answer. In order to explain the American victory, one must first understand how the war was actually waged, how the men of the armies of the Revolution were recruited, what weapons they used, what they wore, how they were supplied. Let us turn our attention to these matters in our survey of the Armies of the American Revolution.

Left: Pennsylvania State Regiment. This regiment suffered more than most from scarcity of equipment throughout the war. In 1776 they were reported to be without shirts, breeches or stockings. In 1778 their commander complained to the Governor of Pennsylvania that unless he received assistance from the Council it would be impossible to clothe and equip his troops properly. Their uniforms were similar to the Hessian allies of the British, which resulted in their being fired upon by their own side on more than one occasion.
Below: The Battle of King's Mountain was one of the operations which delayed Cornwallis' march northward from the Carolinas to Virginia in the last phase of the war.

The Soldiers

In 1775 the total strength of the British Army was some 48,000 officers and men, of whom about 8500 were on the North American continent. This force consisted largely of infantry, with a small amount of accompanying artillery but with no cavalry. By 1781 the British force in North America amounted to 48,647, of whom 39,294 were infantry, 6869 cavalry and 2484 artillerymen. In addition to this mustered force there were several thousand contracted civilians acting as drivers, waggoners, sutlers and general hangers-on and odd-job men.

With all this manpower available, it becomes all the more amazing that the Revolutionary War ended the way it did. To argue, as some do, that a motivated colonist was a better fighting man than a mercenary or uncommitted British soldier is far from a satisfactory explanation. The regular British soldiers of the day——and the vast majority of the British troops in North America were regulars, the hurriedly raised and less well trained troops being retained in Europe——were probably the finest fighting troops of the day. Within a few years of the Revolution's close, many of these same troops were the instruments which broke Napoleon: but the noteworthy difference between the campaigns against Washington and Napoleon lies in the leadership and organization. It is always interesting to speculate on how various events in world history might have gone had some vital factor been altered, and a profitless field of surprise lies in how the War of Independence might have fared had Wellington been in charge of the British forces.

For the root cause of the British Army's poor showing lay entirely with the organization and the command structure. The faults of the commanders have been fairly exhaustively and conclusively exposed over the years; what has been less well documented is the appalling supply problem facing the administration, and the inept way in which it was handled. Almost everything the British soldier ate, wore, rode or fired had to be transported from Britain by ship, since there was insufficient material in the colonies. The administrative machine was split between the

Horse Guards (responsible for Infantry and Cavalry), the Master-General of the Ordnance (responsible for Engineers, Artillery and a wide variety of supplies for other arms), the Commisariat (other items of supply), the Navy Board (responsible for providing shipping and transportation), the Board of Admiralty (responsible for the Royal Navy and for some other aspects of transportation), and many other semi-autonomous agencies such as the Clothing Board and the Board of Survey, all of whom had some vital function which they jealously guarded and all of whom, to a greater or lesser degree, overlapped the functions and responsibilities of some other agency. All of this insured a fine climate for rivalry, obstructionism and strife, and each of the various agencies had time-hallowed and time-absorbing systems of operation and channels of responsibility which proved totally unable to adapt to the needs of the fighting troops and which, in consequence, never managed to produce the results demanded of them.

Take, for example, the provision of guns for the artillery. The Board of Ordnance was responsible for their provision and, upon application from the Secretary at War, would authorize, by a letter to their Principal Storekeeper, the issue of the required number of guns. The Principal Storekeeper would then in turn authorize, again by letter, the weapons to be brought from store, inspected, furnished with the requisite scale of accessories and fitted up with carriages and limbers. On receipt of advice that all this had been done and that the guns were now ready to be issued, he would write back to the Secretary and inform him that the guns were ready at such-and-such a depot and might be collected by a suitably authorized person. If the required guns were in stock this ceremonious procedure might well be expedited in a month or six weeks. But if the guns were not in stock then they would have to be acquired either by withdrawing them from stations to which they had been issued or by manufacture. Either case meant a long delay: in the first case letters had to be written to the out-stations to warn them of the withdrawal; replacement guns had to be found, prepared and issued; the withdrawn guns had to be transported back to store, examined, repaired, and then re-issued. If manufacture was involved, contracts would have to be drawn up with gun-founders, patterns provided, prices agreed, the weapons cast, bored and turned, inspected, marked, proved, and placed in store so that the original procedure could then begin. And how long this might take was a matter for speculation.

Eventually, one way or another, the guns were ready and they would then be collected from the depot in order to be shipped to America. Now the Navy Board had to be approached in order to provide shipping to take the guns from Woolwich, which was usually the issuing depot, to Cork Harbour in Ireland, the assembly point for all transatlantic shipments. On arrival there, the guns and carriages had to be examined and repaired if necessary after their voyage, and then prepared for shipment and parked ready for the next stage of their journey. For this stage the Navy Board had to be approached once again, this time to provide a civil ship, on contract, to carry the stores.

So far the process had been cumbersome enough, but now fresh difficulties arose in the matter of finding a ship and getting it to sail. Merchant ship owners were reluctant to risk their vessels, since the French Navy was active in the Atlantic and the owners were well aware of the trouble they would run into in the matter of trying to claim any sort of compensation from the bureaucratic machinery should their ships be lost. One solution tried was an appeal to the cupidity of the ship's masters by issuing them with Letters of Marque as privateers. Armed with this vital paper they could, should they come across one, capture an enemy vessel and claim its value as Prize Money. Laudable as this policy was, it had the wrong effect; instead of sailing directly across the ocean and delivering their cargoes, numbers of captains took off into the blue on privateering expeditions in search of prizes, the importance of their cargo to the British Army in America meaning nothing when weighed against the chances of a quick profit.

Above: The Count de Rochambeau was one of the most competent military commanders of the war. His professional armies fought with Washington's troops, and both travelled south from New York to Virginia to close in and surround Cornwallis at Yorktown.

Right: The Green Mountain Boys. Originally the frontiersmen of Ethan Allen's patriotic gang, they were formed in 1770 in New Hampshire and Vermont to protect their rights as settlers against officials from New York. They participated in the Battle of Fort Ticonderoga in 1775, after which a new regiment was formed under Seth Warner and called the Green Mountain Rangers; they were assigned to the Army of the North. They achieved a notable victory at Bennington in 1777 during the Saratoga campaign. Their arms were English or French muskets. Some carried American rifles, but all were not equipped with bayonets.

A charge by the Continental Army at the Battle of Monmouth, 28 June 1778, when Washington attacked Sir Henry Clinton's rear guard as they withdrew from Philadelphia to New York after the French joined the war.

Even if the ships were available and the captains trustworthy, the caprices of wind and water militated against any degree of regularity of supply. The failure of the British expedition to Cape Clear in 1776 was largely due to their lack of armament, since the guns which were supposed to accompany the force were still lying in a ship's hold in Cork Harbour, prevented from sailing by a spell of foul weather.

But ordnance was a relatively simple proposition. Far more fragile were the arrangements for the supply of food. In the first place, the contractors who undertook to supply the food to Cork lost no opportunity of providing inferior goods; bad meat, weevilly biscuits and all the other familiar foulnesses of the age. On top of that (which was more or less anticipated, since it had been the practice of contractors since time immemorial), they were not averse to making up casks to the proper weight by placing a substantial layer of stones in the bottom topped by whatever the cask was supposed to contain. Add to this the hazards of poor packaging, pilfering and slow shipment, and the plight of the British soldier in America becomes a sorry one indeed. It was a rare event when the Redcoat received his official allowance of a pound of beef a day, and starvation was a constant threat. When starvation was staved off, scurvy from an unbalanced diet was the alternative, which accounts for the appearance in the shipping manifests and ration returns of the time of hundreds of barrels of sauerkraut. This was not, as has sometimes been suggested, home comfort for the Hessians, but an anti-scorbutic measure for the whole army. Another interesting speculation in the realms of might-have-been is to contemplate the result of issuing 200 barrels of sauerkraut to a British formation during the First or Second World Wars; outright mutiny doubtless, medical opinion notwithstanding.

Indeed the provision of anti-scorbutics at all, in 1775, is remarkable; of course the British forces had appreciated the dangers of scurvy years before. The marvel lies not in the sauerkraut but in its provision, for the Army in the field was conspicuously deficient in anything which could remotely be held to resemble

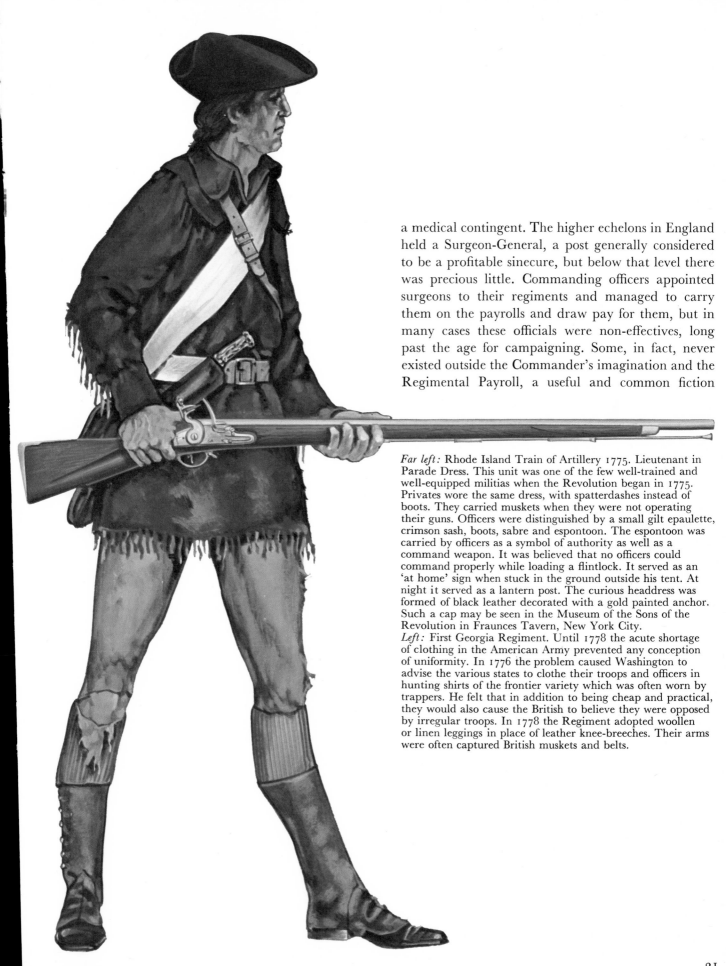

a medical contingent. The higher echelons in England held a Surgeon-General, a post generally considered to be a profitable sinecure, but below that level there was precious little. Commanding officers appointed surgeons to their regiments and managed to carry them on the payrolls and draw pay for them, but in many cases these officials were non-effectives, long past the age for campaigning. Some, in fact, never existed outside the Commander's imagination and the Regimental Payroll, a useful and common fiction

Far left: Rhode Island Train of Artillery 1775. Lieutenant in Parade Dress. This unit was one of the few well-trained and well-equipped militias when the Revolution began in 1775. Privates wore the same dress, with spatterdashes instead of boots. They carried muskets when they were not operating their guns. Officers were distinguished by a small gilt epaulette, crimson sash, boots, sabre and espontoon. The espontoon was carried by officers as a symbol of authority as well as a command weapon. It was believed that no officers could command properly while loading a flintlock. It served as an 'at home' sign when stuck in the ground outside his tent. At night it served as a lantern post. The curious headdress was formed of black leather decorated with a gold painted anchor. Such a cap may be seen in the Museum of the Sons of the Revolution in Fraunces Tavern, New York City.

Left: First Georgia Regiment. Until 1778 the acute shortage of clothing in the American Army prevented any conception of uniformity. In 1776 the problem caused Washington to advise the various states to clothe their troops and officers in hunting shirts of the frontier variety which was often worn by trappers. He felt that in addition to being cheap and practical, they would also cause the British to believe they were opposed by irregular troops. In 1778 the Regiment adopted woollen or linen leggings in place of leather knee-breeches. Their arms were often captured British muskets and belts.

which was all profit. As a result when the poor unfortunate private soldier was wounded, his treatment was usually a rough and ready first aid performed by his comrades, guided by experience in past campaigns, or by one of the 'necessary women' who trailed along at the tail of the regiment.

The 'necessary women' (the expression is the official one used in the records of the time) deserve more than a passing mention. Some of them were the legal wives of NCOs and soldiers: it was customary to allow a proportion of the long-serving men to marry 'on the strength', that is, with their wives officially registered and entitled to rations. The wives were entitled to stay with their husbands on foreign postings, space——a minimum——being allowed for them on the troopships. In return for this official recognition they were expected to act as laundresses, storekeepers, assistant cooks, scullions, and in any other menial capacity which presented itself. But from all accounts, and contrary to what we of today's cynical age might assume, the standard of morality was high. An 'on the strength' wife was a wife, and any libidinous soldier who tried any nonsense was likely to be triced up to the triangle to 'have his back scratched' with the cat-of-nine-tails or to suffer some less official but equally condign punishment from the affronted husband and his comrades.

However, the number of official wives was never sufficient to cope with all the chores, and several women of unofficial status were always to be found following the regiment. Doubtless some of them plied the oldest profession, but even so they did their share of the chores. But once on campaign it was the women, ultimately, who fed, bandaged, succored and nursed the unfortunates; many records speak of the women searching the battlefield after the fighting was over in order to rescue the wounded and identify the dead. And if, at the end of the day, the on-the-strength wife found she was an off-the-strength widow, she usually managed to recover her official status in a short time. There were always plenty of candidates for the dead man's shoes——and bed.

A common epithet employed by contemporary American writers when referring to the British soldier was 'Bloodyback'; in fact, as a nickname, it applies properly to only one English regiment, the Northamptonshires, which was one of the few which did not serve in the North American campaigns. But its use stems from the excessive use of corporal punishment in the British Army of the day. The standard punishment for any but the most trivial of military offences was the 'cat-of-nine-tails', the nine-stringed lash. One hundred lashes was virtually the standard quota, two hundred common; regulations were promulgated from time to time as to the maximum which were allowed to be administered, but in those days of near-autonomy by commanders the regulations were rarely closely observed, and there are records of as many as a thousand lashes being inflicted. It might also be noted that the 'necessary women' were not immune from this form of punishment, generally inflicted for fighting, drunkenness or looting, though the limit was generally three-score 'on the bare doup' instead of across the back.

Although this punishment seems outrageously barbarous today, one should recall that it was, in many ways, a barbarous age, and nobody thought lashing particularly out of the way or tried to read peculiar psychological traits into those who advocated it. Discipline had to be enforced, and with the private soldier's pay standing at a copper or two a day, fines were out of the question. With the Army on campaign, confinement to camp was the normal routine and could scarcely be considered as a form of punishment. And it should also be remembered that crimes which attracted the lash in the Army were frequently ones which carried the death penalty in civil courts; so perhaps the bloodyback had something going for him after all.

Against this background of misery the British soldier played out his allotted role in North America, producing results which, even if not as good as hoped for in England, were certainly far better than his leaders and mentors deserved. What sustained him was little more

Below: General Francis Marion, 'the Swamp Fox', inviting a British officer to share his meal. Marion was one of the best guerrilla fighters of the American Revolutionary War. This illustration was taken from an oil painting by John Blake White which hangs in the Capitol of the United States in Washington.

Left: Prinz Ludwig Dragoons. King George III augmented his forces by hiring mercenaries from petty German princes in the Holy Roman Empire. Regiments were sent to America in the spring of 1776 to assist the British under General Howe in 1776–7 and General Burgoyne in the campaign of 1777. It was customary among the Germans to distinguish their regiments by the name of the Commander——frequently a Prince. Prince Ludwig's Dragoons was the only German cavalry regiment to serve in North America. It arrived without its horses and was obliged to serve on foot, but the soldiers refused to be separated from their long broadswords.
Right: Nathaniel Greene, who was arguably one of the best military commanders in the Continental Army.

than professional pride and that mysterious *esprit* of the British regimental system under which death was a lesser evil than disgracing the Regiment or failing in one's duty to one's comrades.

The American soldier was distinctly a citizen soldier. Not for him the enlistment for life of the regular soldier of the age. His sole object was to enlist, fight, win, and then get back to farming or storekeeping or whatever. This had the usual unfortunate repercussions which inevitably follow from such a point of view, however praiseworthy it may seem. It is an article of faith among uninstructed civilians that the soldier's trade is a simple one and the soldier an ignorant fellow who elects to be a soldier in order to evade the responsibilities of civil life. From this premise it follows that any intelligent civilian, given a rifle, can immediately become a proficient soldier and thus, given sufficient numbers, the war can be over by sunset and we can all go home.

It was ever thus; it is the same today, notwithstanding the technological advances of the age, and it will be the same to the end of time. Which is why citizen forces, militia, guerrillas, resistance movements—— call them what you will——are nothing more than a nuisance and an embarrassment until they finally learn their new trade the hard way or collapse in the process. The two things needed by an armed force to convert it from a rabble to a viable combat unit are training and discipline; and until these two were acquired, most of the hurriedly-raised American forces were of negligible worth. Fortunately for the infant nation, the British commanders failed to appreciate this point; they were also short of troops and anxious to play the whole thing in low key at the outset. As a result, during their months of irresolution the vital training and discipline were imparted, and when the British commanders finally decided to take things seriously the opportunity to knock the infant revolution on the head had gone forever.

Four days after the Battles of Lexington and Con-

A scene from the Battle of Bunker Hill, 16 June 1775, the
first major action of the Revolutionary War. Although the
Americans were defeated, they proved both to themselves and
the British that they had the determination and ability to
fight. The British casualties represented about half of the
striking force used to take the hill and the surrounding
peninsula. Sir Henry Clinton said that another victory like
Bunker Hill 'would have ruined us'.

cord, on 23 April 1775, the Provincial Congress gave the necessary authorization to permit the raising of a force of some 1300 men under the command of Artemus Ward. In the following June Ward was replaced by Washington and the formation of more units put under way. By the following year 28 regiments had been authorized, each of ten companies composed of about 82 officers and men. In 1776 the strength of the Continental Army was set at 88 regiments——about 73,000 men, but this was little more than a pious hope. At its peak, in 1776–77, the Army mustered about 20,000 of all ranks, while at Valley Forge the number sank to less than 5000.

The cause of this fluctuation in numbers can be divided between desertion, sickness, mutiny and the effects of an ill-defined system of enlistment. The terms of a man's enlistment varied between the colonies, and, like many similar schemes in other wars and places, reflected the boundless optimism of the civilian soldier that the war would soon be over once he personally got involved in it. One year was considered onerous, and enlistment from three or six months was more common. There was no saving clause about the duration of the war, and as a result when his enlistment period was up the soldier smartly reverted to civilian life, standing on no formality and often simply walking out of camp and heading for home when he felt that his duty had been discharged.

The progress of the war also affected morale to an extreme degree; when things looked good, men flocked to enlist. When things went wrong they were equally prompt to desert, though it must be said that they usually came trooping back to re-enlist when the tide of fortune turned.

Another source of trouble was the question of pay; the American soldier was paid somewhat better than the Redcoat, but instead of respectable and respected coin, he was paid in Continental banknotes, which were regarded with some suspicion by tradesmen who were far from sure that the war would result in independence and the notes redeemed in specie. Furthermore the war, as always, caused scarcities and led to inflation, so that the small pay became less and less useful. This led to a number of mutinies of varying seriousness at different times, as well as adding fuel to the fire burning under the deserters.

As far as sickness was concerned, the Continental Army ran the same hazards as the King's men, and with just about the same level of medical and sanitary organization. There was also the addition problem that hygiene and sanitation are difficult matters to knock into an undisciplined force, so that in the early days the liability to sickness was rather greater than in the British Army.

All these evils gave General Washington ample cause for sleepless nights, and he soon realized that the root of most of the trouble lay in the prevailing amateur approach to soldiering. Some units refused to serve under any officers but their own; the officers themselves were frequently voted into office by the men, and one can safely assume that military ability would be a minor factor in selection under such a system. Moreover, the egalitarian attitudes fostered by the revolution ran counter to the basic tenets of military discipline. If the corporal felt he was as good a man as the captain, he was likely to question the captain's assessment, disagree with his orders, and eventually disobey, to either do nothing or else follow his own course of action, either way leading to confusion if nothing worse.

By 1778 Washington despaired of ever reasoning with the various elements of his army, so he appointed Baron von Steuben as his Inspector-General. Von Steuben was a Prussian who had learned his trade in the most highly trained and ferociously disciplined army of the age, that of Frederick the Great. Frederick had inherited this force from his father, and on to the basic discipline he had overlaid a system of drill and tactics which covered almost every eventuality, until he had a force which was well-nigh unstoppable. Many countries adopted his system of tactics and training, frequently misapplying them in the process, but von Steuben was intelligent enough to extract what was needed and discard the more extreme and

repressive portions which would not have sat well upon revolutionary shoulders. The rather extemporaneous organization of the Continental Army was modified to produce sub-units of a size more suited to maneuver; regiments were now split into eight companies each of about a hundred men, and two companies were taken as a tactical unit, since this was as much as one man could hope to command by voice and control in battle.

With the Continental Army at last on the way to a semblance of organization and efficiency, it is all the more surprising to contemplate the proliferation of Provincial Militia units which existed alongside it and which nominally supported it. The whole question of Militia versus Regular forces——in any country—— during the 18th and 19th centuries is a vexed and involved one which cannot be explored here at any length, but it involved a great deal of political give-and-take in which military efficiency was often ignored. The basic question was one of raising men rapidly. In order to accomplish this, local areas were encouraged to raise troops, usually by appointing a prominent local personage to be the Commanding Officer (without reference to his military knowledge or lack of it) and then relying on parish patriotism to fill the ranks. The system produced the desired number of bodies, but their efficiency was questionable. Like the fabled little girl, when they were good they were very good . . . but more often they fell somewhat short of the desired standard, largely due to the same old story of democracy versus discipline. When the unit was run as an extension of the parish meeting, morale was good while efficiency was low. As soon as any sort of rigid discipline and training was introduced, the easy-going, club-like atmosphere evaporated and the desertion figures rocketed. Similarly, while the campaign resembled a summer picnic, all was well, but once life became more spartan many of the picnickers decided that the hearth held more attractions than the camp-fire. As a result the Militia units were of varying efficiency and reliability, and it is a matter of record that Washington was reluctant to put too much dependence upon them, preferring to use them as occupational and garrison troops while the brunt of the battles were taken by the trained troops of his Continental Army.

In the matter of dress, the American forces were rarely in agreement. In the beginning, of course, the Minuteman turned out in whatever he happened to be wearing at the time. The few regular colonial forces in existence were clothed in uniforms closely resembling the standard British pattern, due to their original place in the British Colonial Forces. As the Continental Army came into being, attempts were made to devise a suitable mode of dress, but with each Provincial Assembly keen on distinguishing its own troops by some form of distinctive dress, little was achieved in the way of standardization. In 1775 the Continental Congress recommended that all uniform coats be of brown, with each regiment distinguished by the color of facing on the lapel and the provision of numbered regimental buttons. Brown was selected since it was an easily-procured and common dye, but it proved impossible to specify a particular shade of brown, and coats ran the gamut from deep cocoa to light beige, depending upon the source of supply of the dyed cloth.

Many units adopted the traditional hunter's dress of buckskin, since it was practical and, as Washington himself pointed out, it carried a psychological advantage in that 'it is a dress justly supposed to carry no small terror to the enemy who think every such person a complete marksman'. But buckskin was not an article in sufficient supply to allow the whole army to be so equipped, and this idea had to be given up. Eventually, in 1779, a General Order laid down the mode of dress, specifying blue coats with various colors of facing for different regiments; but in 1782 this was changed once more to provide red facings for heavy infantry and white facings for light.

In spite of Washington's best endeavors and Congress's orders, no uniformity was ever achieved before the end of the war, and it is scarcely surprising. The supply of such staples as food and powder was difficult enough, and as long as the soldiers were serviceably

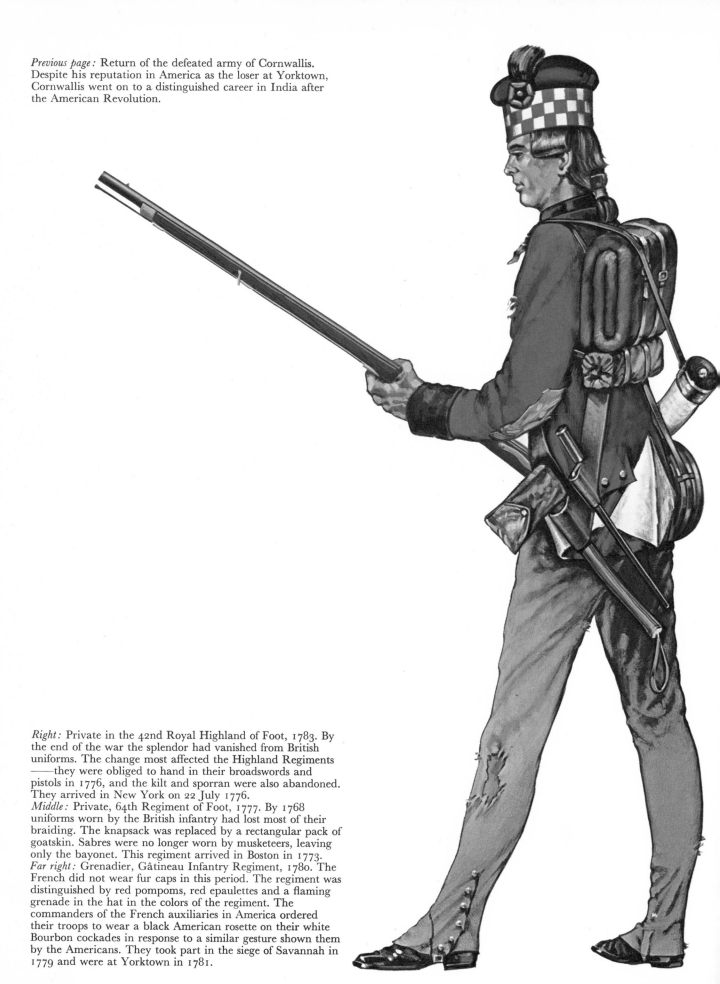

Previous page: Return of the defeated army of Cornwallis. Despite his reputation in America as the loser at Yorktown, Cornwallis went on to a distinguished career in India after the American Revolution.

Right: Private in the 42nd Royal Highland of Foot, 1783. By the end of the war the splendor had vanished from British uniforms. The change most affected the Highland Regiments ——they were obliged to hand in their broadswords and pistols in 1776, and the kilt and sporran were also abandoned. They arrived in New York on 22 July 1776.
Middle: Private, 64th Regiment of Foot, 1777. By 1768 uniforms worn by the British infantry had lost most of their braiding. The knapsack was replaced by a rectangular pack of goatskin. Sabres were no longer worn by musketeers, leaving only the bayonet. This regiment arrived in Boston in 1773.
Far right: Grenadier, Gâtineau Infantry Regiment, 1780. The French did not wear fur caps in this period. The regiment was distinguished by red pompoms, red epaulettes and a flaming grenade in the hat in the colors of the regiment. The commanders of the French auxiliaries in America ordered their troops to wear a black American rosette on their white Bourbon cockades in response to a similar gesture shown them by the Americans. They took part in the siege of Savannah in 1779 and were at Yorktown in 1781.

Left: Rifleman, 1st Pennsylvania Rifle Battalion, 1775. The 1st Battalion were stout, hardy men, many over six feet tall. They favored the hunting shirt of the rifleman. The rifle was more accurate than the musket. Its disadvantage was its slowness of loading and lack of bayonet, leaving the men defenseless against the sort of charge at which the British excelled.

Right: Gunner, 4th Battalion, Royal Artillery, 1777. The Royal Artillery saw action in America throughout the entire war, and they arrived in New York in July 1773. The traditional blue coat has been worn ever since. The 4th Battalion, for reasons unknown, was authorized to wear a black feather in their hats. The hair was powdered and 'clubbed' (turned up at the neck). Their general appearance was quite similar to that of the American artillerymen.
Below: Molly Pitcher leading American troops at Monmouth, New Jersey in the battle fought there in 1778. Her legend far exceeds her role in the battle.

clad in something which could not easily be mistaken for a British uniform on the field of battle, that was good enough.

Cavalry contributed little to either side during the War of Independence. The British fielded only two regiments, the 16th Queen's Light Dragoons and the 17th Light Dragoons, and eventually the 16th transferred their effective men and horses to the 17th to form a single reinforced regiment. The reasons for this lack of equitational enterprise were mixed; in the first place the American campaign was not being conducted on the lines of formal European-style massed battles in which a large cavalry force could, by their weapons and speed, make a decisive contribution. In the second place, the troop horses had to be shipped across the Atlantic, and enough has been said already about the difficulties of transportation to make it abundantly clear that this was a considerable obstacle. Even if the

Left: Queen's Rangers, a famous and active corps, first known as 'Roger's Corps'. The tall black leather hats bore the Corps badge on the front——a small white metal crescent with Queen's Rangers engraved on it. The feathers of green and white had black added after the death of Major André. The epaulettes were of interwoven chain. Riflemen were equipped with musket and bayonet. The green uniform was inconspicuous——most suitable for light troops. Other loyalists or provincial corps also wore green. The tall hat was adopted to avoid confusion with the American forces.
Right: Minute Men, 1775. Some of the first soldiers of the Revolution, they were given their name because they were expected to be ready at a minute's notice to serve the Revolutionary cause. The Minute Men fired 'the shot heard round the world' at Lexington which opened hostilities in Britain's American colonies.

horses arrived in America their subsequent movement was a massive problem. When General Clinton mounted his expedition to South Carolina in 1779 he lost all his horses on the voyage from New York to Charleston due to the lack of proper transport ships and facilities. In 1777 General Howe lost a large number of horses during shipment from New York to Philadelphia; his quartermasters provided forage for a voyage of 21 days, but due to adverse weather the journey took 40 days. Many horses died of starvation

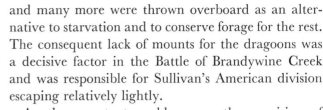

and many more were thrown overboard as an alternative to starvation and to conserve forage for the rest. The consequent lack of mounts for the dragoons was a decisive factor in the Battle of Brandywine Creek and was responsible for Sullivan's American division escaping relatively lightly.

Another constant problem was the provision of forage for all the horses which, of course, ate their heads off whether they were fighting or not. These various factors led to the cavalry being principally employed in reconnaissance and scouting roles. On occasions, the shortage of mounts led to the dragoons having to dismount and fight as infantry.

In the Continental Army cavalry formed a relatively minor branch. Washington was an infantryman and had little conception of the wider functions of cavalry beyond reconnaissance. Moreover, he was probably somewhat soured by his first brush with the horse soldiers. In 1776 the Connecticut Light Horse arrived at Washington's Headquarters and, like most cavalry militia of the time, felt themselves to be a cut above the common herd, since they were largely enlisted from the scions of the local gentry. Their idea of a trooper's life appeared to alternate between gallant dashes into a demoralized enemy and peacocking before the local belles. Such things as cleaning stables, procuring fodder, standing guard and acting as couriers were beneath their dignity, and after a short experience with these Elegant Extracts, Washington felt that he could survive without them and sent them back to Connecticut.

By 1777 though, the lack of a mobile arm was making itself felt, and Congress authorized the formation of four cavalry regiments. The establishment was loosely based on that of the British Light Dragoons and consisted of 360 officers and men organized into six troops. As with other intentions, this one never reached full fruit since there were never enough horses to put the entire strength into the saddle at any one time. There was no shortage of volunteers——they were better paid than the infantryman, and there are always people who find it glamorous to gallop around the battlefield on the back of a nag——but the lack of horses meant that most of the men finally fought as foot soldiers. Moreover, the dearth of mounts meant that the regiments could never act as a shock striking force, so that what mounted elements there were spent their time scouting and doing reconnaissance duties. Only in the Southern campaigns did the cavalry approach their full potential, largely due to the distance from Washington, the more ready availability of horses, and the excellent leadership of their commanders.

Cornwallis Retreating!

PHILADELPHIA, April 7, 1781.

Extract of a Letter from Major-General *Greene*, dated CAMP, at *Buffelo Creek, March 23, 1781.*

"ON the 16th Inftant I wrote your Excellency, giving an Account of an Action which happened at Guilford Houfe the Day before. I was then perfuaded that notwithftanding we were obliged to give up the Ground, we had reaped the Advantage of the Action. Circumftances fince confirm me in Opinion that the Enemy were too much gauled to improve their Succefs. We lay at the Iron-Works three Days, preparing ourfelves for another Action, and expecting the Enemy to advance : But of a fudden they took their Departure, leaving behind them evident Marks of Diftrefs. All our wounded at Guilford, which had fallen into their Hands, and 70 of their own, too bad to move, were left at New-Garden. Moft of their Officers fuffered—Lord Cornwallis had his Horfe fhot under him. Col. Steward, of the Guards was killed, General Howard and Cols. Tarlton and Webfter, wounded. Only three Field-Officers efcaped, if Reports, which feem to be authentic, can be relied on.

Our Army are in good Spirits, notwithftanding our Sufferings, and are advancing towards the Enemy; they are retreating to Crofs-Creek.

In South-Carolina, Generals Sumpter and Marian have gained feveral little Advantages. In one the Enemy loft 60 Men, who had under their Care a large Quantity of Stores, which were taken, but by an unfortunate Miftake were afterwards re-taken.

Publifhed by Order,

CHARLES THOMSON, Secretary.

§†§ : Printed at N. Willis's Office.

Left: 1st Continental Regiment of Light Dragoons, previously known as the Virginia Light Dragoons. They were raised in Virginia in 1775 under Colonel Theodorick Bland. They were familiarly known as the 'Virginia Horse' in the Continental Army. The uniform shown, that of Bland's own troop, was brown faced with green; other companies had blue coats with red facings. They wore leather breeches and top boots, helmets of black leather with a green turban, and long, flowing white horsehair crests. First armed with only sabres and pistols, after 1777 they had carbines or short muskets as well. They served in the Yorktown siege.

Above: Posters like this encouraged the Americans that the British forces of Cornwallis had little chance of escape.

Right: Iroquois Indian Scout, 1775–82. The Indians were badly treated by many Americans, and they transferred their allegiance from the French to the British after the French were beaten in the Seven Years War, or the French and Indian War, as it was known in America. They were not much help to the British, but they were a terror to the Americans on the frontier. In 1777 General Burgoyne employed the Iroquois in New York State with some effect, but the Americans devastated their settlements and forced the Iroquois, Munsees and Senecas to seek refuge in British forts, while the Delawares unconditionally surrendered. When the war ended the Indians were abandoned by the British, except in the Northwest Territory, where they were continually supplied by British arms, sent in from Canada or from the key forts along the Great Lakes which the British refused to abandon.

Below: 'Gathering of the Mountain Men', by Lloyd Branson.
Right: 17th Regiment of Light Dragoons, 1775–83. The quality
of this regiment made it the first cavalry corps to be
dispatched to America. It left Ireland in 1775 and landed in
Boston just before the Battle of Bunker Hill. After the British
retreat from Philadelphia in 1778, the 16th Light Dragoons,
the only other British cavalry regiment in the war, transferred
to the 17th. The combined regiment was known as the
'Queen's Dragoons'. Its headquarters were at Hempstead,
Long Island from 1778 to 1783. Helmets of brass with long,
red horsehair crests of red silk turbans around the base were
worn. Front plates painted black often had a badge and
motto——a death's head with the legend 'or glory'. Coats
were red with white facings, and buckskin breeches and black
top boots were worn.

41

Top: German Jäger rifle. It was extremely accurate and was used in competitions until the 1850s.
Above: An American-built .62 calibre rifle.
Below: A scene from the siege of Yorktown, as one of the last British redoubts was taken.

Muskets & Rifles

The shot which echoed across Lexington Green on that fateful April day two hundred years ago, and which was, in the immortal phrase, 'heard round the world', has been the source of some contention ever since. Was it fired from the ranks of Parker's minutemen? Or Pitcairn's infantry? Or from the sidelines? Or from a window in the nearby tavern? Was it an incensed farmer who fired? An exasperated Redcoat? Or, as has been suggested by some eminent authorities, an agent of Sam Adams seizing the opportunity to put a match to the powder train which eventually exploded into Revolution?

No matter; we will never know, and at this remove of time it is of little consequence. But what we can say with some amount of certainty is what sent the fateful bullet on its way; there can be little doubt that the weapon which fired the shot was a flintlock musket. So we might as well begin our tour of the weapons of the War of American Independence by considering the flintlock shoulder weapons of the day.

By 1775 the flintlock mechanism was at its highest peak of perfection, a reliable and efficient means of ignition in trained hands. But it was not quite so simple to use as is commonly believed, which accounts for General Washington's preoccupation with training the Continental Army. Enthusiasm is no substitute for training and discipline, as Washington well knew. His adversaries were probably the best trained troops in the world at that time, and to face a British volley with equanimity and perform the manifold evolutions of loading a muzzle-loading flintlock and firing it with some hope of hitting demanded a high degree of training and application which didn't come naturally to most men.

To understand this better, let us look first at the mechanics of a typical flintlock musket. The barrel, secured in the wooden stock by pins or bands, was a smooth-bored tube, closed at the rear end by a screwed, and possibly welded, plug. On the right-hand side of the stock, at the rear end of the barrel, was the lock mechanism. Now the parts of the mechanism have undergone various changes in name since they were

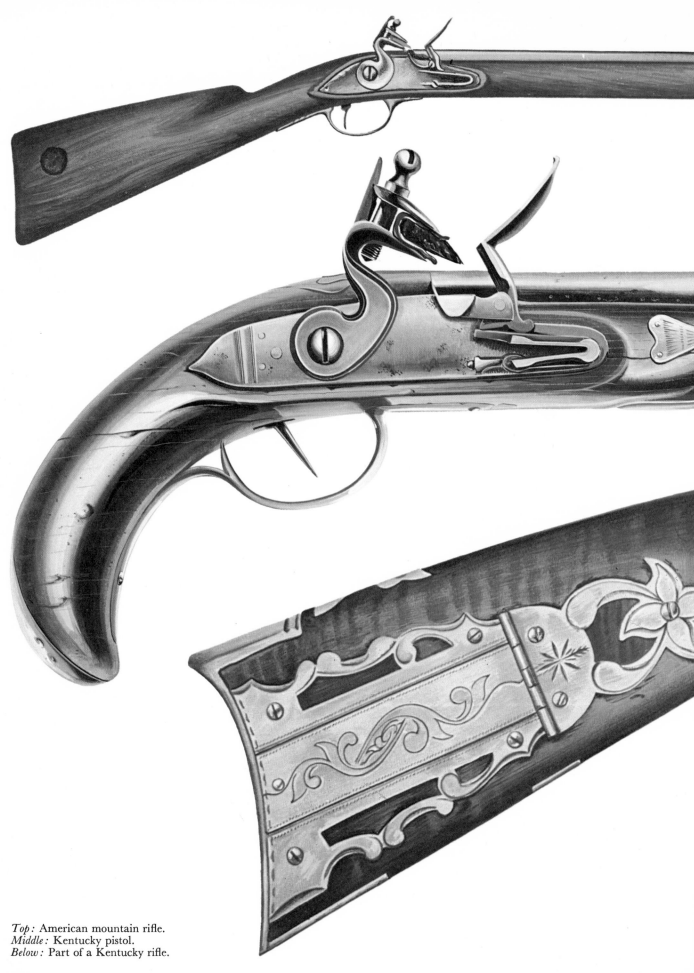

Top : American mountain rifle.
Middle : Kentucky pistol.
Below : Part of a Kentucky rifle.

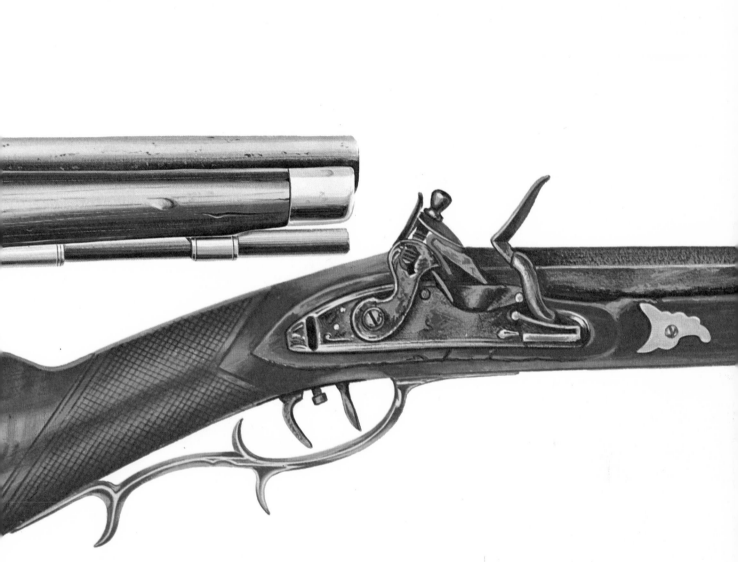

in everyday use, and for the sake of accuracy and in order that the description relates to the contemporary extracts which will follow, let us be precise and call things by the names the Minutemen called them.

The lock consisted of, firstly, the *Cock* (nowadays called the hammer) which held between its jaws a piece of flint. The cock was under pressure from the mainspring and controlled by the trigger. When pulled back by the firer's thumb against the pressure of the mainspring, the cock was held by the trigger, and when the trigger was pulled the cock flew forward so that the tip of the flint described an arc.

In front of the cock was the *pan*, connected to the interior of the musket breech by a narrow passage called the *vent*. The pan was normally covered by a piece of metal which, after forming a cover to the pan, turned upwards in an arc designed to intersect the fall of the cock. This upturned section, which is today known as the frizzen, was, in 1776, known confusingly as the *hammer*, and its purpose was to cause sparks to be struck upon contact between it and the falling flint. Due to the accurate shape of the hammer, the impact of the flint drove it forward, hinging so as to open the pan cover and thus allow the sparks to enter the pan, igniting the gunpowder in the pan and thus flashing through the vent to fire the powder in the musket's breech.

How did the gunpowder get there? Listen to the British official *Exercise of the Firelock* of the time:

'Upon the command "Prime and Load", make a

quarter face to the right . . . at the same time bringing down the firelock to the priming position, with the left hand at the swell, the side-brass touching the right hip, the thumb of the right hand placed in front of the hammer with the fingers clenched, the firelock nearly horizontal. Open the pan by closing the elbow to the side . . .

Upon the command "Handle Cartridge"; 1st, draw the cartridge from the pouch. 2nd, Bring it to the mouth, holding between the forefinger and thumb, and bite off the top of the cartridge.

On the command "Prime"; 1st, shake out some powder into the pan and place the three last fingers on the hammer. 2nd. Shut the pan by closing the elbow. 3rd. Seize the small of the butt with the above three fingers.

Upon the command "About", turn the piece nimbly round to the loading position, meeting the muzzle with the heel of the hand, the butt within two inches of the ground and the flat of it against the left ankle . . .

2nd; Place the butt on the ground without noise, raise the elbow square with the shoulder, shake the powder into the barrel, putting in after it the paper and ball.

3rd. Drop the right elbow close to the body and seize the head of the ramrod. . . . Upon the Command "Draw Ramrods"; 1st force the ramrod half out and seize it back-handed exactly in the middle . . .

2nd. Draw it entirely out . . . turning it at the same time to the front, put it one inch into the barrel.

Upon the command "Ram down Cartridge"; 1st. Push the ramrod down till the second finger touches the muzzle.

2nd. Press the ramrod lightly towards you and slip the two fingers and thumb to the point, then grasp as before.

3rd. Push the cartridge well down to the bottom.

4th. Strike it two very quick strokes with the ramrod.

Upon the command "Return Ramrods"; 1st. Draw the ramrod half out, catching it back-handed. . . .

2nd. Draw it entirely out . . . turning it to the front; put it into the loops and force it as quickly as possible to the bottom. . . . after a pause . . . bring the firelock with one motion to the same position as the word "Prime and Load" . . .

Upon the Command "As Front rank, Ready". Place the thumb of the right hand on the cock and fingers behind the guard, and cock the piece; then take a grasp of the butt, fixing the eye steadily upon some object in front.

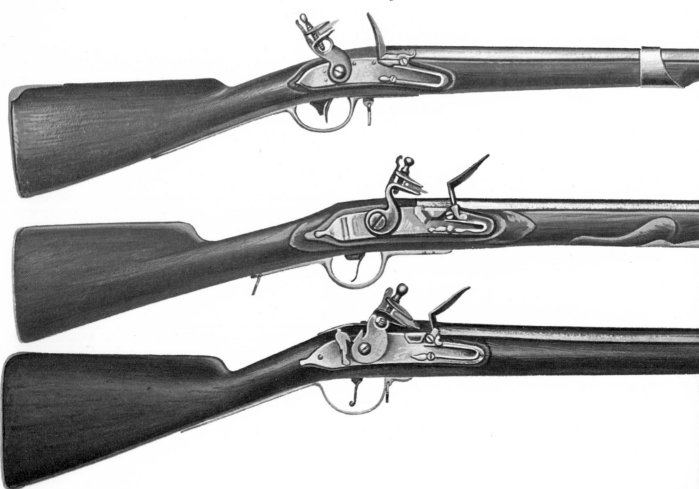

Right: François Joseph Paul de Grasse, the Marquis de Grasse-Tilly, later Count de Grasse. This great French admiral led the French Navy to victory in the Chesapeake which blocked the British escape route from Yorktown.
Below: French infantry musket.
Middle: German infantry musket.
Bottom: English doglock musket.

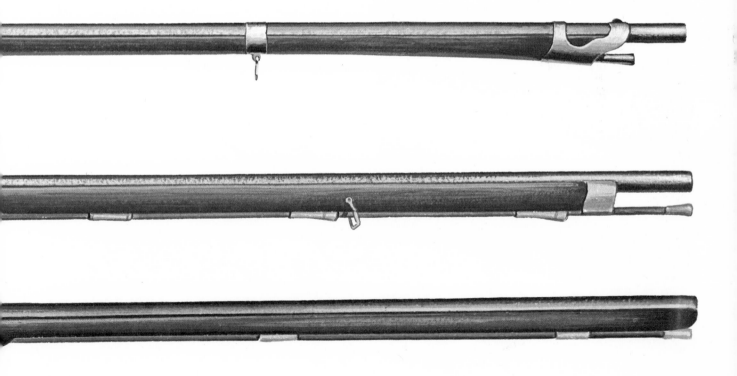

Below: English dog lock musket; detail of the lock.
Bottom: Detail of a German infantry musket.
Right: Detail of a French infantry musket.
Right below: Spanish Miquelet pistol lock.

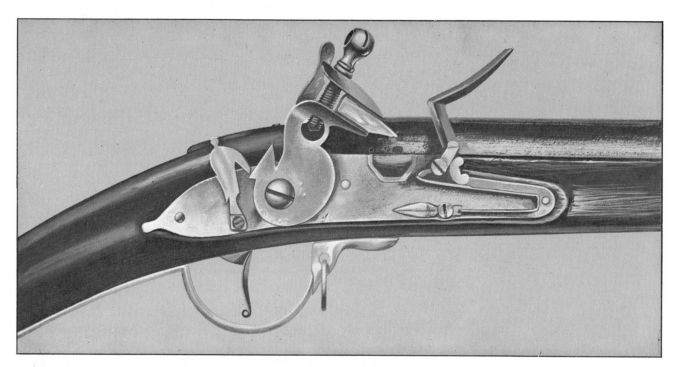

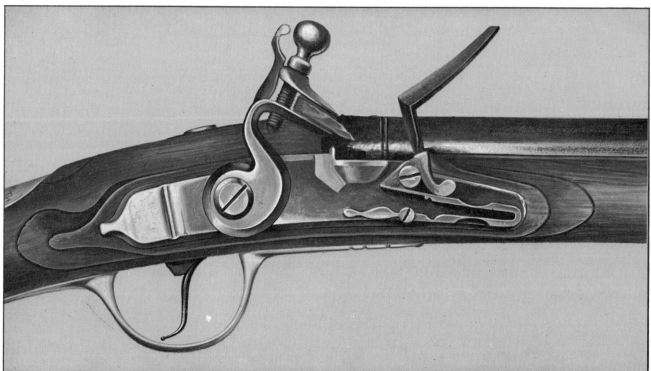

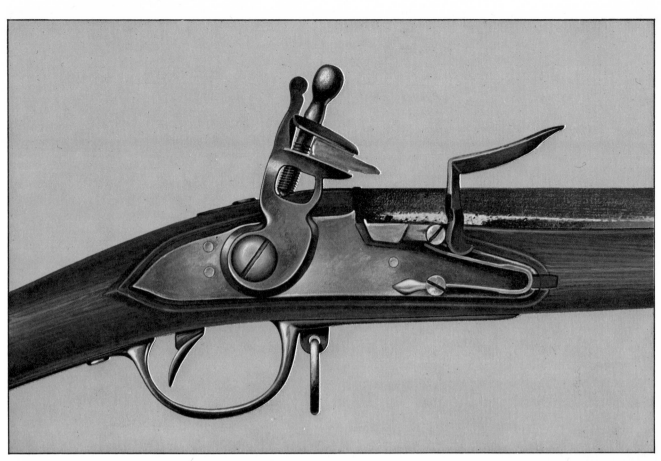

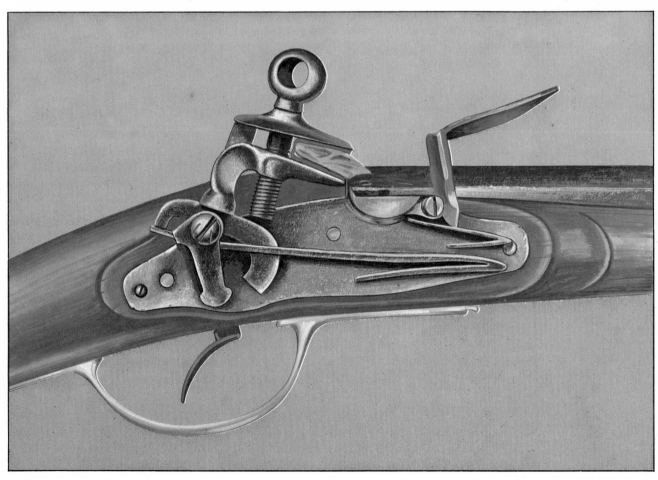

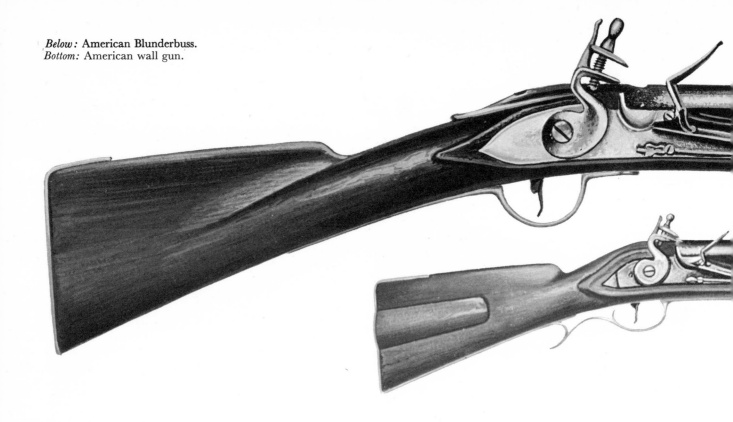

Upon the Command "Present". Bring the firelock up to the present slowly and independently until in line with the object the eye had fixed upon; then pull the trigger without a jerk, and when fired remain looking on the aim until the word "load" is given.

Too much pains cannot be taken to prevent the recruit from raising his firelock with a jerk; it must be deliberately raised until aligned with the object that the eye is fixed upon and so that he may lay the right cheek on the butt without too much stooping of the head; particular care must be taken that the recruit in this position shuts the left eye in taking aim, looking along the barrel with his right eye from the breech pin to the muzzle.

Upon the command "Load", bring down the firelock to the priming position and take hold of the cock with the thumb and fingers behind the guard, and draw it back to half-cock. The loading will be performed as before directed.'

One must, of course, bear in mind that this is the drill manual for the recruit; once trained, and in action, the commands would merely be 'Prime and Load' followed after a short pause by 'Present', the intermediate stages being run through in sequence without the intervening commands being given. Even so, it makes firing the M1 rifle look like child's play, and Washington's insistence on training becomes more understandable. But before that stage of perfection could be reached, there were a number of minor points which had to be driven home. First the soldier had to be able to aim the firelock:

'When the recruit has attained a perfect knowledge of the Platoon Exercise he is to be carefully habituated in TAKING AIM. To this great object too much care and attention cannot be devoted; it is the means by which the soldier is taught to fire with precision, or, in other words, to kill his enemy; and it cannot be too strongly inculcated that every man, who has no defect in his eyes, may be made a good shot at a fixed object. . . . The true principles upon which correct shooting may be taught are extremely simple; they are to be found in the natural connection that exists between the hand and the eye. . . .'

Moreover, the matter of fitting a flint into the firelock was one of critical importance:

'The recruits must be individually taught the true principles which direct the fixing of the flint. In fixing flints, no uniform mode should be attempted; the flat side must be placed either upwards or downwards according to the size and shape of the flint and also according to the proportion which the cock bears in height to the hammer, which varies in different muskets. This is observed by letting the cock gently down and

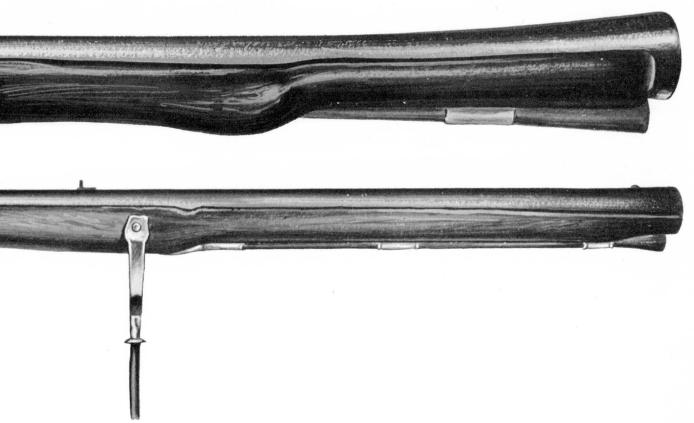

observing where the flint strikes the hammer, which ought to be at the distance of about one-third from the top of the hammer. Most diligent observation ought at the same time to be made whether every part of the edge of the flint comes in contact with the hammer, so as to strike out fire from the whole surface. A flint will often appear to the eye to be well and skillfully fixed, and to stand firm and square, yet on trial being made as above-directed, it will prove to have been very ill-fix't, inasmuch as the surface of the hammer on some muskets does not stand square, but stands a little aslant to the cock. Each particular flint, therefore, requires its own particular mode of fixing so as to accommodate itself to the particular proportions and conformations of each particular lock. In whatever position the flint should be, it must be screwed in firmly; two pieces of very soft lead, which will embrace the flint, are recommended to ensure this. And the cock should be let down to ensure the flint passes clear of the barrel.

Whenever a piece has been fired, the first opportunity should be embraced of examining whether the flint remains good, and fixed as it ought to be, and no time should be lost in correcting whatever may be found amiss. . . .'

After mastering these essential points, the next step vas to accustom the recruit to the peculiar sequence of

events when he actually pulled the trigger. The first time you see a flintlock fire, the flash and smoke are so spectacular that the individual components go unnoticed, but after becoming used to it, the attentive observer can make out, quite distinctly, three separate stages: first, the flash of the flint as it strikes the hammer; then the explosion of the priming in the pan; and a sensible interval later, the ignition of the propelling charge——the actual firing of the musket. Because of this sequence, there is an instinctive reaction in the inexperienced firer: the explosion of the priming causes him to flinch, disturbing his aim, so that when the charge fires a split second later the musket is no longer properly aligned with the target. In order to overcome this tendency, the recruit was initiated gradually:

'The recruit having acquired the habit of readily aligning the firelock with any object selected by the eye, he will next be taught to burn priming without winking, or the slightest degree altering the composure of his countenance. . . . The instructor must watch the recruit minutely in this practice, which must be continued until the eye is perfectly indifferent to the flash caused by the ignition of the powder.'

After this he graduated to firing blank cartridges:

'The recruit in loading is to be instructed to shake the powder well out of the cartridge and to ram the

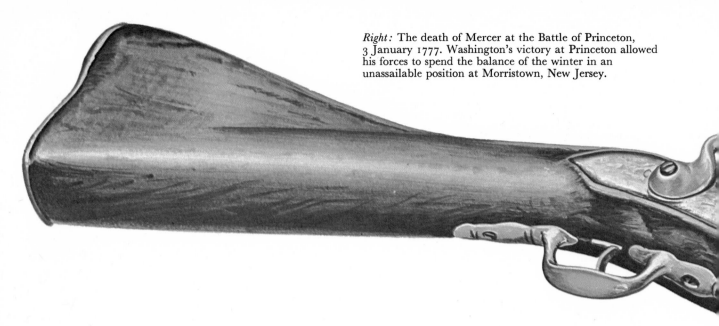

paper as wadding home. The instructor will fire each recruit singly by word of command, minutely observing that he fires with perfect composure of countenance and steadiness of body, wrist and eye . . . The practice with blank cartridge must be continued until the recruit becomes perfectly firm and motionless at the explosion and recoil, without which it would be a mere waste of ammunition to commence firing with ball.'

It is interesting to note the mention of recoil in this context; in modern times the idea of training with blank cartridges is expressly forbidden for the very reason that blank ammunition does not give recoil and thus gives the recruit a false impression, but a well-wadded charge of gunpowder could give sufficient recoil to provide the recruit with very nearly the real thing.

Only after he was perfectly habituated to the flash and smoke did the recruit begin to use ball ammunition; and then in such a way as to give him confidence in his own ability:

'The ball cartridge is scrupulously reserved for the purpose of *proving* the recruit's progress or proficiency in shooting; with this view, three or four ball cartridges are given to him and he is placed before a target, which in the first instance should be round and eight feet in diameter, at the distance of thirty yards or even nearer, so that it will be impossible for him to miss it. This method is intended to produce confidence in the young soldier and to show him that his firelock will carry true if accurately aligned. . . .'

The muskets used in this fashion during the War of Independence were many and varied; the long arms of the British Army during this period——indeed, during any period prior to the percussion era——are not amenable to simple classification. While the French had already begun to classify weapons to their nominal date of introduction into service and, between the introduction of specific models, stick fairly rigidly to their specifications, such a system was unknown in England. The reason behind this was largely the peculiar British system of procurement and supply. While the French had established government arsenals to turn out weapons to an approved pattern, the British system relied entirely upon commercial manufacturing facilities.

Having decided upon a new weapon, the Board of Ordnance would then have a specimen made by a gunmaker, and his specimen would then become the 'Sealed Pattern' by virtue of having attached to it a linen label which bore, in wax, the seal of the Board. This sealed pattern was then deposited with the Board and was available for contractors to examine, so that they could see what they were letting themselves in for. It also acted as the comparative check in that any weapon delivered to the Army could be taken and compared with the Sealed Pattern Arm. Any divergence from the pattern could result in the weapon being refused or, if it was a relatively minor divergence, the price being 'abated', that is reduced by a percentage reflecting the degree of non-compliance with the pattern. This system of 'Sealed Patterns' survives in British service to this day, and covers everything from cap-badges to cannon; for small arms there is still the 'Pattern Room' at the Royal Small Arms Factory, Enfield Lock, in which all the sealed patterns are deposited and stored.

Having sealed the design, the Board of Ordnance would then negotiate contracts with various manufacturers for parts of the firearm——not for the whole weapon, for the gun trade in England did not work

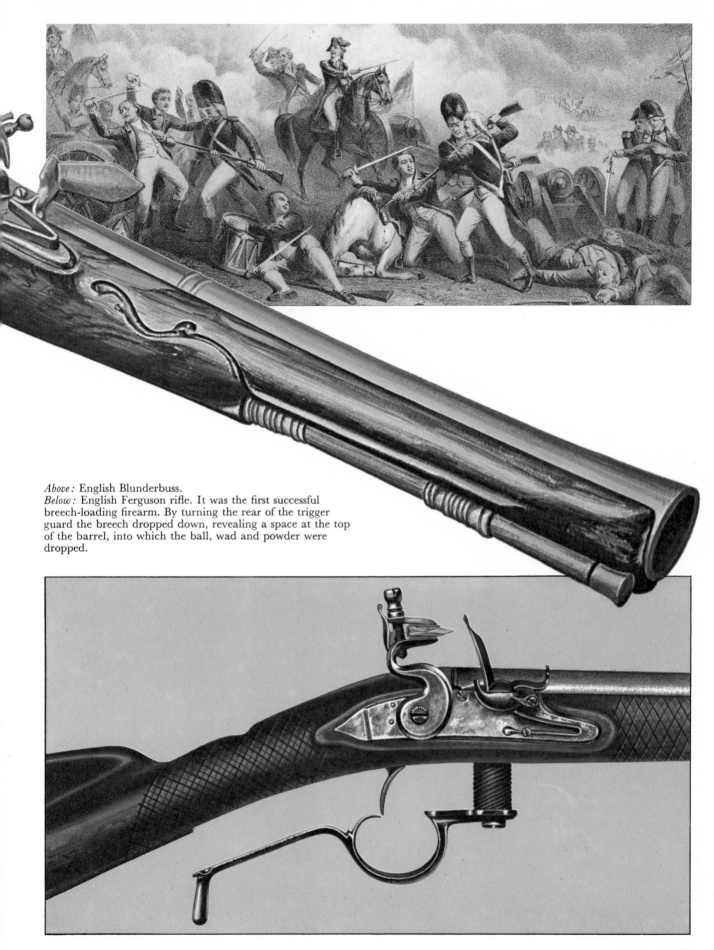

Above: English Blunderbuss.
Below: English Ferguson rifle. It was the first successful
breech-loading firearm. By turning the rear of the trigger
guard the breech dropped down, revealing a space at the top
of the barrel, into which the ball, wad and powder were
dropped.

Right: Ferguson rifle, one of the most important weapons of the war.
Below: Washington, in his camp before Yorktown, asks the British emissary sent by Cornwallis for a cessation of hostilities.

that way. Specialists in lock-making, stock-making, barrel-making and furniture-making all worked separately. Their products went to a 'stocker', who then assembled and finished the complete weapon. This was the system for the making of commercial firearms, and since these were the only facilities available, the same system had perforce to apply to the manufacture of military arms. Consequently the Board issued contracts for locks, barrels, furniture (the various fittings such as butt plates, trigger-guards, barrel bands, ramrods and so forth) and stock wood in sufficient amounts to make up the desired quantity of arms——a figure which generally reflected the amount of money the Board had available, and not necessarily the military or political considerations of the time.

The contractors would then deliver their completed items to either a designated store depot or to the central depot, the Tower of London, where the incoming items were all examined, checked against the sealed pattern, and either accepted or rejected. From there batches of components sufficient to make up a specific number of weapons were sent out to contractors known as 'Stockers and setters-up' generally located in London close to the Tower, where the weapons were then delivered to the Tower of London armories, checked, proved, and placed in store against the time they were needed.

One thing will be obvious from this description of the system is that there will be inevitable minor differences between weapons of nominally the same pattern. Even working from the Sealed Pattern and the drawings furnished by the Board of Ordnance, small differences in dimensions occurred from job to job, and each maker was bound so have his own idiosyncracies which reflected themselves in the constructional details of his work. So that while any one weapon was basically the same, minor differences between individual guns could and did occur, and these must be accepted as a result of the system and not adduced as differences in pattern. A further source of variation in weapons lies in the system of returning

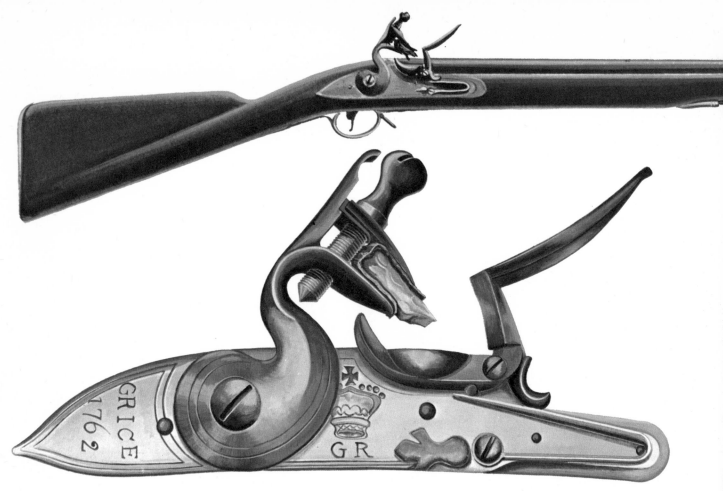

firearms to the Tower from time to time for inspection, refurbishing and repair, during which components which were worn could be replaced, sometimes with items of a newer or improved pattern, leading to some odd combinations of components in a seemingly standard weapon. This can lead to difficulty when a student is attempting to place a date on some weapon, basing his assumptions on some feature of the lock or furniture. Until 1764 locks were stamped with the date of acceptance, which is reasonably accurate, although subsequent change of lock can throw this system adrift; after 1764 it is practically impossible to be more accurate than the nearest ten years or so, and attempts to tie a weapon down to a particular year are misplaced, to say the least.

The standard British Army firearm of the period was the Brown Bess or Long Land Service Musket.

Introduced during the reign of Queen Anne (1702–14), its adoption has been attributed to the urgings of the Duke of Marlborough, but it seems to have taken some time to get into production after being officially approved for service, since the earliest dated specimens known are marked 1720. The origin of the nickname is shrouded in mystery; indeed, there is doubt as to when the expression was first used. It has been suggested that 'Brown' is due to the walnut stock, earlier service weapons having had the stock painted black. A more likely explanation is that it comes from the brown color of the steelwork, due to a chemical treatment given as a rust preventive measure. As to 'Bess', some historians have tried to extrapolate this back to tie it with Good Queen Bess herself, which is stretching things a little far; the good lady had been dead for over a hundred years before the weapon was

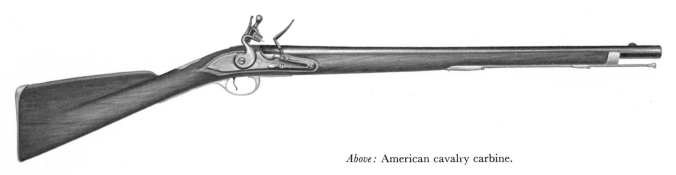

Above: American cavalry carbine.

56

Above: English Brown Bess musket.
Left: Lock of the Brown Bess musket.

adopted. More likely the name allied itself to 'Brown' by alliteration's artful aid; 'Brown Phyllis' or 'Brown Sophia' would have smacked of the ridiculous, but 'Brown Bess' has that ring of companionability which in later years produced 'Long Tom', 'Big Bertha' and the Grease Gun.

Another theory, which I put forward with some diffidence, is that the name came, by way of substitution, from another immortal 'Bess' who came to prominence early in the life of the musket; Dick Turpin's famous horse 'Black Bess'. Turpin, the notorious highwayman, was hanged in 1739, and the rough soldiery of the day may have derived some amusement in naming their muskets in a manner analogous to Turpin's horse.

The Long Land Service Musket was of .753-inch calibre and had a 46-inch barrel; it fired a 490 grain lead bullet by means of a 124 grain powder charge (though one should remember that a small portion of that charge went into the priming pan). The weapon was heavy at 11¼ lbs, but the thought uppermost in the designer's mind was robustness and reliability on service when the Redcoats were liable to serve in any corner of the globe, far from the resources of an armorer's shop. Its effective range was considered to be 200 yards, and within that limitation it was about as accurate as any smoothbore could be expected to be; it is noteworthy that the final test of marksmanship for the trained soldier of the time was firing at an eight-inch diameter bulls-eye at 200 yards range. The bullet was somewhat smaller than the barrel calibre, about .70 inch in diameter, so that it would load easily and quickly down a barrel fouled after prolonged firing, and this windage between bore and bullet meant that shooting was bound to be erratic, since the actual path of the ball through the air depended largely upon which side of the barrel it happened to touch as it left the muzzle.

In the middle 1760s the Long Land Service Musket was supplemented, and then gradually replaced, by the Short Land Service Musket——which was still known as 'Brown Bess', to the confusion of later students. This cut the barrel down to 39 inches and the propelling charge to 70 grains, though the weight of the weapon was only reduced by two ounces. This produced a better-balanced and more handy weapon which became the standard British long-arm until it was replaced by a percussion musket in 1842. Even then it continued to plague Americans, since the obsolete weapons were sold to Mexico and were used by them in the 1846–47 campaigns of the Mexican War.

Other muskets were also in service in varying numbers during our period. The Sea Service Musket, nominally for naval use, found its way into some army formations when the supply system fell over its feet and muskets of the Brown Bess pattern were not available. The dimensions of the Sea Service musket tend to vary; nominally the barrel was 42 inches long, but specimens with barrels as short as 36 inches have been seen. The most obvious difference between these and the 'Brown Bess' pattern lies in the finish to the steelwork; the Sea Service muskets, strange to relate, have the metalwork either burnished bright or blackened chemically, and as a result are

Above: French cavalry carbine.

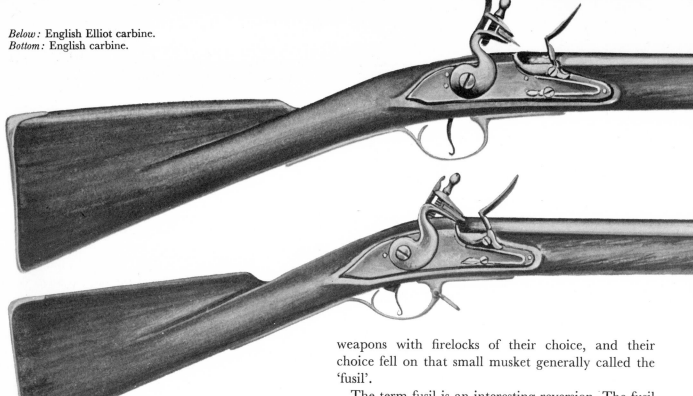

Below: English Elliot carbine.
Bottom: English carbine.

referred to as being either 'Bright' or 'Black' models. Considering the notorious corrosive qualities of sea air, one would have expected the best possible rust-proofing process to be applied universally.

Slightly older than the Sea Service was the Marine and Militia Musket; this was another 42-inch barrel pattern, generally with the metalwork blackened, and with some very small changes in the furniture. The most readily observable change is the fixing of the top tang of the butt-plate with a screw into the stock, something never done with the Brown Bess patterns.

As will be noted later, the official weapon for officers and senior NCOs of the day was an edged weapon, either the spontoon or the halberd. However, the American campaigns before the start of the War of Independence showed that carrying such things on the field of battle was tantamount to bearing a large sign saying 'Shoot Me', since bearers of such symbols of authority became prime targets for sharpshooters. As a result the practice arose (as it re-emerged in later wars) of officers and NCOs arming themselves with the same weapon as their men, so as to be indistinguishable from a distance. Eventually the practice was recognized officially, and weapons for this purpose were produced. It was obviously impossible to expect the flower of the aristocracy to cart an eleven-pound Brown Bess around in the field, and officers were permitted to replace their edged

weapons with firelocks of their choice, and their choice fell on that small musket generally called the 'fusil'.

The term fusil is an interesting reversion. The fusil was, in effect, the first military flintlock, selected troops (called Fusiliers) being armed with them while the bulk of the army were still armed with matchlocks. Some historians ascribe the term to Vauban, the famous French fortress-builder and engineer. Vauban had an inquiring mind and was never averse to delivering an opinion on anything which took his fancy. In a letter to Louvois, the Minister of War, in 1687, he condemned the current matchlocks and urged the provision of *fusils mousquet*, flintlocks modeled on those used by buccaneers of the day. Doubtless Vauban wrote the letter, but, as in many fields outside his specialities, he was ill-informed; the first record of fusiliers appears to be about 1643, and the British Army had formed the Royal Fusiliers two years before Vauban put pen to paper, so he cannot be credited with inventing the term 'fusil'.

But the fusils which now appeared in the hands of British officers were not simply flintlock muskets; they were generally privately made arms several pounds lighter than the issue musket and of high quality, although there do appear to have been a small number procured through the usual Board of Ordnance channels. Generally speaking all these officers' fusils had barrels about 36 inches long, calibres between .66 and .70, and they weighed between six and a half and seven and a half pounds.

The dividing line between the fusil and the other class of light flintlock, the carbine, is difficult to draw with any exactitude since the parameters were much the same and some weapons adopted either title at

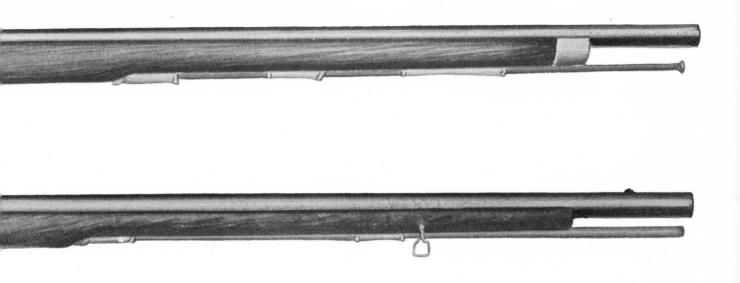

different times in their lives. Generally, carbines were lighter than muskets and formed part of the equipment of cavalry, being also issued to officers and NCOs of some infantry regiments——whereupon they were called fusils. A strict definition is almost impossible; some carbines had barrels as long as contemporary muskets; the calibre generally called 'carbine bore'——0.65 inch——found application in other weapons as well, while carbines were made in other calibres. Construction too was no criterion; it all depended on what that sort of weapon was being called when the pattern seal was applied and the title inscribed on the label.

The earliest standard carbine in British service, the Light Dragoon Carbine, was little more than a Short Land Service Musket under a different name. This was replaced in a few years by another weapon, also called the Light Dragoon Carbine, which had a 36-inch barrel and carried one feature which is generally accepted as identifying cavalry carbines—— a 'sling bar' on the left side of the stock, opposite the lock. This sling bar was used, as its name implies, to anchor the sling in such a fashion that it tightened under the weapon's weight and thus was less likely to allow the carbine to swing about and get in the rider's way. It became a notable feature of most cavalry carbines for many years, certainly until the practice of carrying long arms in saddle-buckets took over.

Another model is identified as the Artillery and Highlander's Carbine. Issued in 1757, this has a barrel of full 42-inch length and generally resembles a full sized musket, but it can be distinguished from the issue muskets of the time by its generally lower standard of manufacture. It has been suggested that

as the artillery were rarely called upon to fire shoulder arms and the Highland regiments were prone to get to grips with the enemy using a broadsword, a lower quality weapon was perfectly satisfactory for them.

A rare case of foot soldiers being issued with a carbine was in the case of the light infantry companies. From 1770 onwards they were issued with the Light Infantry Carbine——though just to confuse matters it was sometimes referred to as the Light Infantry Fusil——of .67 calibre. This, though, was as far as it went; the length of the barrel was still 42 inches. The stock was thinned down slightly and some minor changes made to the furniture, so that the weight came out at just over seven pounds, which was a worthwhile saving. Another version had a .65-inch bore and appears generally to be little changed from the Short Land Service Musket, though the weight had been reduced to eight pounds.

A more drastic redesign was the 'Elliott' carbine, officially introduced in 1773 and produced in Ireland. This was of the usual carbine calibre, .65 inch, but was drastically shortened, the barrel being only 28 inches long and the weight just over six pounds. This was issued to some light cavalry units; one of these was the 17th Light Dragoons, and a number of Elliott carbines accompanied them to America. The first models, designed by General Elliott as a private venture for his 15th Light Dragoons in about 1760, were stocked to the muzzle and specimens often have 'GEN. ELLIOTT'S DRAGOONS' engraved on the barrel. After gaining official acceptance in 1773 a second version was produced, recognizable by having a peculiar fore-end cap and a ramrod with a gracefully shaped handle. The stock finished some distance short of the muzzle, and the

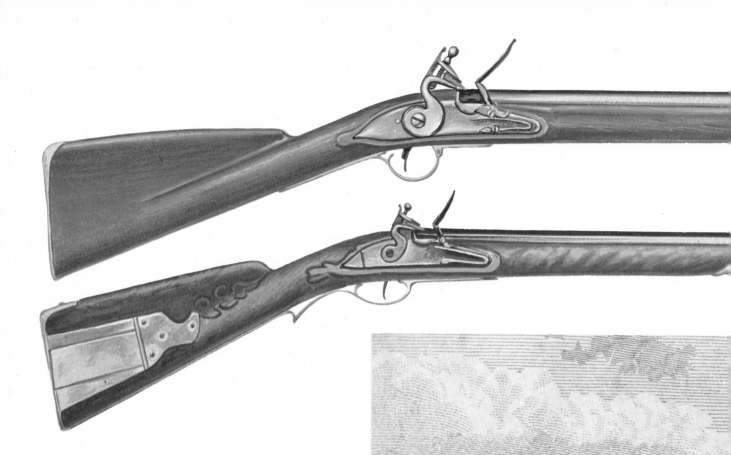

ramrod clipped into the fore-end cap by a groove cut beneath the ramrod handle.

Finally, in this review of the shorter long arms, it would be unfair to miss out a couple of the more outlandish developments. The first, which stemmed indirectly from the War of Independence, was due to General Burgoyne. After his defeat at Saratoga he returned to England to be quizzed by Parliament on the affair; having satisfied them as to his lack of blame he was appointed to command of the 23rd Light Dragoons. He forthwith designed, and persuaded the Board of Ordnance to approve, a 'musketoon for cavalry troops'. Due to its bell-mouthed barrel it soon got the name of 'Burgoyne's Blunderbuss', though it was not intended as any sort of scatter-gun. It was, in fact, an extremely short carbine, with a barrel only $16\frac{1}{4}$ inches long, the bore being the standard .65 inch. One hundred of these weapons were made and issued to Burgoyne's regiment, but it is doubtful that any managed to cross the Atlantic before the war ended. While Burgoyne was gently ridiculed for this design at the time, he seems to have had the right idea. A weapon as short and handy as this would be a far better proposition for mounted troops than the usual pattern of carbine or musket. But the experiment seems not to have been given much attention by the Board of Ordnance, and the musketoons were eventually replaced by standard patterns of carbine and disposed of; few exist today.

Above: American fusil musket.
Below: American rifle.
Bottom: French engraving of the surrender of Burgoyne to Horatio Gates at Saratoga in 1777.

The other out-of-the-way weapon is rather better known; the Nock Volley Gun. Although the name of Nock is always associated with it, it was actually the invention of one James Wilson, and he offered his design of seven-barrelled gun to the Board of Ordnance in 1779. Wilson probably had the American campaign in mind when he offered the weapon, but the Board felt there was little use for such a weapon in land service and passed it to the Board of Admiralty for their observations. The Navy were impressed, doubtless due to their contemporary tactical concept of getting as close to the enemy as possible and then letting fly with all the firepower available, a theory into which the volley gun fitted quite nicely. Henry Nock made his entry on the scene by virtue of being one of the premier gunmakers of the day. He was asked by the Navy to make up some specimens of the Wilson design for trial, and he produced a number of rifled models. These passed their trials well, and contracts were placed forthwith with Nock for a supply of guns; early models were still rifled, though in later years smooth-bored versions were issued, since they were cheaper to make and just as effective.

It will be appreciated that instead of the usual piecemeal system of contracting the Navy gave Nock the whole weapon to build——since these had to be fairly precisely constructed. Nock, of course, took care to engrave his name on every one of them, which is why they have gone down in history as Nock guns. The name of Wilson is almost forgotten.

The volley gun consisted of one central barrel surrounded by another six. The normal flintlock mechanism was used to fire the central barrel, and from the chamber of this barrel radial vents passed to the chambers of the surrounding barrels. Thus, on pulling the trigger all seven barrels fired virtually at once, which must have been a chastening experience for the man holding the thing, since each barrel was .52 calibre. Two batches of guns appear to have been produced, the first dating from 1779 and consisting of 500 guns, and the second, begun in 1787, of only 100. There are some minor differences in the lock

mechanism and the appearance of the furniture between the two models, but in basic construction they remained the same, using 20-inch barrels.

Brown Bess's traditional adversary throughout its career was, of course, the French service musket, the 'Fusil d'Infanterie', a weapon which came in a wide variety of modifications and sub-types. Between 1717, the year of its introduction, and 1777, there were ten different models of infantry musket, plus another 17 variations for use by officers, artillery or cavalry. It is generally called the 'Charleville' musket, from the arsenal at Charleville which produced large numbers, but in fact Charleville did not begin manufacture until the advent of the Model of 1763, and many other arsenals, such as Maubeuge, St. Etienne and Versailles were also concerned with manufacturing the weapon.

The French musket was slightly lighter than the British, due largely to using a .69 calibre barrel of rather thinner section, together with a lighter and more graceful stock. Originally the barrel was secured to the stock by pins, but the 1728 model introduced barrel bands instead of pins; this allowed the stock to be made even lighter until the arm weighed about 9¾ pounds; 59¾ inches long, with a 44¾ inch barrel, it fired a ball weighing about 450 grains.

While the Brown Bess and the Charleville were the primary smoothbore muskets of the period, a few others found their way to America. One such was the enormous .80 calibre Prussian Musket, some of which appeared in the hands of the Hessians and from there found their way to the American side. Five feet in length, with a 43-inch barrel, it weighed slightly under eleven pounds. There were also a number of Dutch muskets, purchased by the British for use by Hessian and Brunswick units during a period of shortage of their own Brown Bess Weapons, and numbers of these have survived in America; they differ in details from standard military weapons of the day but most can be identified by British official stampings. Finally, of course, there were enormous

Above: Dutch military rifle.
Below: Francis Marion, whose guerrilla tactics harassed British forces during their march north through the Carolinas during the last stages of the war.

quantities of 'Trade Pattern' muskets owned by settlers as their personal arms and purchased from all sorts of sources, and a tabulation of all the variations on this theme would be impossible.

But once an American Army began to be raised in earnest, a standard pattern of musket was imperative. It mattered little to a New England farmer if his musket happened to have a bore of .63 or .72 or some other odd calibre, governed entirely by the boring bit which happened to be handy when the gunsmith made the weapon. The farmer made his own bullets in a mould provided by the same gunsmith, and his expenditure of ammunition was negligible compared to his ability to mould more during his non-hunting periods. The provision of ammunition for a military force however, with the expenditure to be expected in battle, was not something which could be left to the individual, and a standardized calibre and bullet was an economic necessity. In July 1775, therefore, Congress passed resolutions to set standards for the muskets to be provided by the various Committees of Safety, underlining their demands by a further resolution passed in November which said, in part, 'that it be recommended to the Colonies that they set and keep their gunsmiths at work to manufacture good firelocks with bayonets. Each firelock to be made with a good bridle lock, of three-quarter-inch bore and of good substance to the breech. The barrel to be three feet eight inches in length, the bayonet to be eighteen inches in the blade, with a steel ramrod . . . the price to be fixed by the Assembly or Convention or Committee of Safety of each Colony.'

It will be seen that the calibre (.75 inch) and the barrel length (44 inches) approximated to the British Long Land Service Musket, and generally speaking, Brown Bess was taken as the pattern. After all, it worked for the Redcoats so it ought to work equally well for the Minutemen. There is, moreover, always a good case to be made out for having weapons of the same calibre as your adversary, since it simplifies ammunition supply; if you need more, go out and steal some from the other side.

But with the intervention of the French came supplies of the Charleville musket, and this gradually replaced Brown Bess as the pattern for the Committee of Safety weapons. Not only was it lighter, a factor of some significance with irregular forces, but it appears to have been credited with having a slight edge over Brown Bess in accuracy, due to the somewhat lesser windage between ball and bore. Above all there was an attractive economic advantage; the smaller bore demanded a smaller bullet, and the saving in lead amounted to a whole pound of that scarce metal in every hundred balls cast.

The musket was the workhorse of the Revolution. Its advantages lay in its robustness, its rapidity of fire——for in spite of the involved drill previously quoted, a trained soldier could get off four shots a minute——and its devastating effect at short range, fired in massed volleys from close order ranks of troops. It is grossly unfair to say, as some have done, that the musket was only of use in order to provide a handle for the bayonet. Had that been so the unwelcome complications of drill and ammunition supply would gladly have been abandoned and the soldiers provided with pikes. But the weapon which fable associates most with the War of Independence is the rifle, though in truth there were relatively few of them used.

The rifle had been born in Europe many years before. The earliest reliable reference appears to be as early as 1498 and mentions the practice of cutting straight grooves in the barrel in order to reduce trouble from powder fouling. There is no record of the identity of the genius who first thought of spiraling the grooves, but specimens of arms with twist rifling exist which are reliably dated as early as 1542. The Danish Army first adopted rifled weapons for military use; a wheel-lock rifle of .62 calibre with six grooves, dated 1611, is in the Royal Artillery Museum in Woolwich, London. But on the whole the rifle was a hunter's weapon, since the process of loading was much slower than that required for a musket due to the need to force the ball into the rifling to a greater

or lesser degree. Some riflemen used a boxwood mallet and wooden punch to engrave the bullet into the rifling at the muzzle before using the ramrod to force the ball down to the chamber, while others preferred to use a smaller ball, making it fit tightly into the rifling by means of a cloth patch.

Whatever the system the net result was the same ——the bullet left the muzzle spinning, so that it was gyroscopically stabilized. Since it was a tight fit, the caprices of the musket ball, whose path depended upon how it happened to oscillate up the barrel, were eliminated and the firer could be a good deal more confident about where his bullet was likely to go. The only thing he had to worry about was the drift to one side due to the spin of the ball. Why it drifted wasn't satisfactorily explained until the end of the next century, but the shooter of the 18th century knew that it did drift and that he had to aim off accordingly. Some of the more expensive hunting rifles actually offset their sights in order to try and compensate, although this could only be accurate for one particular range, and trying to compensate for

something you don't really understand is at best a makeshift. One other advantage enjoyed by the rifle was a greater range and velocity, due again to the tight fit of the ball. The musket ball's windage allowed a proportion of the propelling gas to rush past and be wasted in muzzle blast, whereas the rifle ball, firmly lodged in the rifling, sealed all the gas behind it and extracted every available scrap of performance from the powder.

The rifle reached America during the early years of the 18th century as German, Swiss and Bohemian gunsmiths emigrated to the New World and set up in business. They found business good, for the frontier dwellers soon saw the advantage of the rifle, for both feeding themselves and their families and also for protection against the various predators of the forest, both two and four-legged. These rifles were generally called 'Jäger' rifles, from the German word for hunter, and were heavy weapons with 7-grooved 30-inch barrels of large bore——between .5 and .7 were the usual calibres. Such heavy-barrelled rifles made excellent practice and were well suited to a day's

Left: Cartoon of General Rochambeau reviewing his French troops. Neither Washington nor Cornwallis considered them to be a laughing matter when they sailed down Chesapeake Bay to join the fireworks display around Yorktown in 1781.

hunting in Europe, but the frontiersman's hunting trip was usually a more prolonged and strenuous affair and he soon began to demand lighter weapons. As a result, the American rifle evolved. Again, economics had a hand in it, since a smaller calibre killed just as dead and saved powder and lead into the bargain, and both these items were scarce and expensive. So the American rifle calibre gradually crept down to about .45 inch, while the barrel was thinned and lengthened to give both better accuracy and more efficient combustion of the charge. Certain other characteristics appeared; maple wood became the standard material for the stock, particularly the Curly Maple which was more durable, took a better finish and had a grain structure which gave a distinctive beauty to the weapon. The stock and butt gradually became more graceful and the butt was provided with a cavity, covered with a sliding plate, to hold spare flints, patches and cleaning equipment. This was in due course superseded by a hinged plate, since the sliding pattern showed a tendency to loosen with use and slide at the wrong moment, losing the contents of the cavity in the undergrowth. These cover plates were frequently highly ornamented.

The majority of the gunsmiths specializing in these weapons settled in Pennsylvania, Lancaster County being frequently quoted as the birthplace of the American rifle, and for this reason the pattern is frequently spoken of as the 'Pennsylvania Rifle'. This is doubtless correct, but the name that sticks to them, and always will, irrespective of the findings of historians, is the 'Kentucky Rifle'. They were not, however, known by that name in 1776; it seems that it was not until the War of 1812 that popular ballads about the Battle of New Orleans brought the expression into general use by drawing attention to Andrew Jackson's 'Kentucky Mountain Men' and their rifles. At the time of the Revolution they were simply known as rifles or long rifles.

The accuracy of the American rifle was legendary; one contemporary report speaks of the ability of frontiersmen to put eight consecutive shots into a five by seven inch target at sixty yards. Even more convincing is the testimony of a man who had more than once found himself on the wrong end of one. Major Hanger of the British Army, later captured at Saratoga, made an official report on the American use of rifles in which he stated his opinion that the average American marksman could hit an enemy in the head at 200 yards, and he further asserted that 'if an American rifleman were to get a perfect aim at 300 yards at me standing still, he would hit me unless it was a very windy day . . .' Which is more than could be said of a lot of draftees armed with far more sophisticated weapons during the Second World War.

The British had already met the frontiersman and his rifle during the French and Indian wars, and realizing the need to fight fire with fire obtained some Jäger rifles from Germany and organized light infantry rifle companies. One British officer went so far as to design a rifle of his own, have a number manufactured and issued, and then take them to war. This was Lieutenant-Colonel Patrick Ferguson of the 71st Highlanders who, adopting an earlier French idea, developed a breech-loading rifle using a vertical screw breech-block operated by a lever forming the trigger guard. Patented in 1776, one hundred rifles were made and used to equip a light infantry company which Ferguson then took to America. The rifle was extremely successful, being particularly noted for its high rate of fire due to the breech-loading feature.

The first major engagement for the Ferguson rifle was destined to be its last——not from any defect in the rifle. Ferguson and his Light Company were part of a diversionary attack at Brandywine Creek on 11 September 1777; they acquitted themselves well until Ferguson was struck in the arm by an American bullet. With the moving spirit removed from the field, the Light Company was dispersed and the rifles disposed of, and Ferguson's experiment ended. He later recovered from his wound, but before he could make a start toward reconstituting his rifle company he was killed at the Battle of King's Mountain, and the Ferguson rifle was never revived.

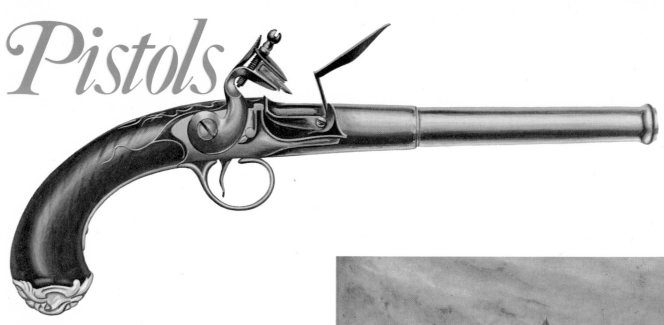

Pistols

As with long arms, the contemporary pistol was a flintlock and came in a wide variety of patterns. They were, however, in less general use than were muskets and rifles, being confined, in regular forces, largely to officers and cavalry. One reason for this was their size and weight; the usual method of carriage was in saddle holsters, the belt holster not having been developed, since such an arrangement for the pistols of the day would have been unduly cumbersome. The only method of carrying pistols on the person was by means of a belt hook, a long metal leaf on the stock opposite the lock. This could be slipped over a sash or belt to suspend the pistol, but such an arrangement was more common among naval personnel, who needed to carry pistols while boarding an enemy vessel and preferred to have both hands free——one hand for the sword and one for the ship.

The flintlock pistol was, so far as mechanism went, little more than a shortened musket. It used the same pattern of lock and was usually fully stocked to the muzzle, the barrel being secured by pins or bands. The muzzle was often slightly flared or bell-mouthed in order to facilitate loading rapidly, which followed exactly the same routine as practiced with the musket. It was the loading problem, as much as anything, which restricted the pistol's use, and it was also the reason for pistols generally coming in pairs. When one was at close quarters, the usual pistol range, there was unlikely to be time or opportunity for reloading, so the first shot had to take effect since it was likely to be the only one. And if it didn't have effect it was likely to be the firer's last. Possession of a second pistol gave a hundred percent increase in firepower. As a result of these considerations the pistol was less in evidence during the years of the Revolution than it was, say, a

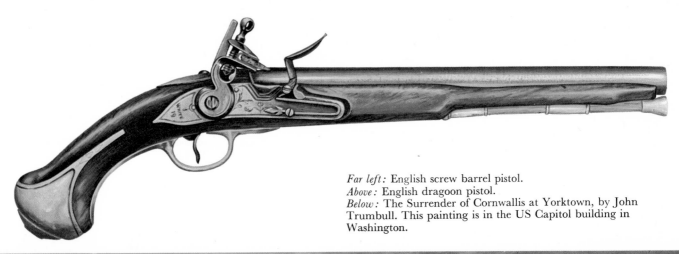

Far left: English screw barrel pistol.
Above: English dragoon pistol.
Below: The Surrender of Cornwallis at Yorktown, by John Trumbull. This painting is in the US Capitol building in Washington.

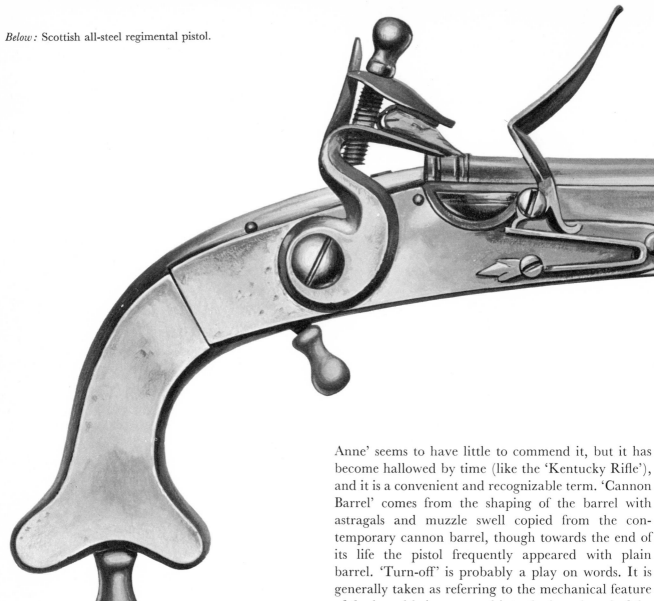

hundred years later and several hundred miles further west. By that time the revolver and the metallic cartridge provided a multiple shot and rapid reloading facility which made the pistol a more practical proposition for a man who was literally laying his life on the line every time he reached for his gun.

While the heavy military pistols were the principal weapons of battle, there was one other class of pistols which deserves mention, since many officers carried them both in and out of battle——the pocket pistol. These were genuinely intended to be carried in the pocket, although one should bear in mind that the pockets of the 18th century were generally more capacious than those of today. The pistols were small, flint-locked, with wooden butts and an unstocked barrel. They go by a variety of names; Queen Anne, Cannon Barrel, Turn-off pistols——sometimes a combination of these names. The designation 'Queen

Anne' seems to have little to commend it, but it has become hallowed by time (like the 'Kentucky Rifle'), and it is a convenient and recognizable term. 'Cannon Barrel' comes from the shaping of the barrel with astragals and muzzle swell copied from the contemporary cannon barrel, though towards the end of its life the pistol frequently appeared with plain barrel. 'Turn-off' is probably a play on words. It is generally taken as referring to the mechanical feature of the barrel being screwed into the breech end of the weapon, from which it could be unscrewed——or 'turned off'——and removed in order to load, which seems logical enough. But there is also the point that in the 18th century——and indeed in some parts of England until the 20th century——'turn off' was synonymous with 'execution'. For example, Jack Sheppard was 'turned off' at Tyburn by the hangman. And since many gentlemen carried a brace of pocket pistols as a precaution against highwaymen and footpads, the weapons may have been nicknamed for their ability to 'turn off' a felon without the formality of arrest and trial.

As originally developed the Queen Anne pistol was more or less of the same basic layout as any other flintlock, but during the course of its life various improvements made their appearance. Thus, fairly early on in the 18th century the lock ceased to be mounted on a separate plate attached to the stockbutt, and a combined breech end and lock unit developed,

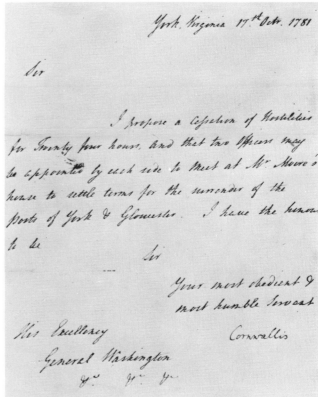

York Virginia 17th Octr. 1781

Sir

I propose a Cessation of Hostilities for Twenty four hours, and that two Officers may be appointed by each side to meet at Mr Moore's house to settle terms for the surrender of the posts of York & Glouchester. I have the honour to be

Sir

Your most obedient & most humble Servant

Cornwallis

His Excellency General Washington &c. &c. &c.

a design which allowed the pistols to be rather smaller and certainly more elegantly put together. The second major step was the redesign of the lock mechanism in its entirety, moving it from the side of the weapon to the center. Again, this made for a neater pistol and also gave the gunsmiths a good deal of scope for individual ideas and a chance for some fancy decoration on the now-matching sides of the pistol. One thing which the move made more difficult was sighting the weapon, since the hammer and cock now interfered with the line of sight along the axis of the barrel. But since pistols in those days never carried any form of sight anyway, and since aiming was largely a matter of instinct, it was a small defect. However, this was the reason that centrally-fitted locks never appeared on shoulder arms.

Queen Anne pistols were, of course, commercial products, and as a result they gave their makers ample scope for individual attention. Ornate butt-caps, engraving of the barrel and chamber, the cock and hammer, and the trigger-guard, of applied escutcheon plates and, in the side-lock models, of the lock and lockplates. All these opportunities were seized, and as a result this class of pistol ranks among the most graceful and beautiful of the arms of this period.

British regulation pistols were invariably large holster types. The Light Dragoon Pistol was authorized in 1756 and had a ten-inch carbine-bore (0.65 inch) barrel. This model, weighing 2½ pounds, was super-

seded in 1759 by a modified version using a nine-inch barrel and weighing somewhat less. This model is distinguishable by the absence of the elongated straps running from the butt cap on the early model, as well as by one or two minor variations. It remained in service throughout the period of the Revolution, although a number of small modifications made their appearance as time went by, notably the thickening of the stock to produce a more robust article.

The Heavy Dragoon Pistol was larger, using a 14-inch barrel of .60 calibre in the first version. This was then changed by shortening the barrel to twelve inches and altering the calibre to .66 or .68, though some versions were as large as .72 inch. After this 'transition period' around the 1750s the design finally settled down to a 12-inch .56 calibre barrel, which remained the standard for some years, at least until the end of the century. All these various patterns were in use in America at one time or another, and the provision of the correct bullets must have been another problem to the already overworked supply organization.

While the Dragoon Pistols were standard issue for cavalry troops, officers of other arms who were habitually mounted were expected to provide their own pistols. It might be noted that this remained the practice in the British Army until the Second World War; while issue pistols were available, officers could provide themselves with any pistol they fancied, the only proviso being that their chosen weapon had to

71

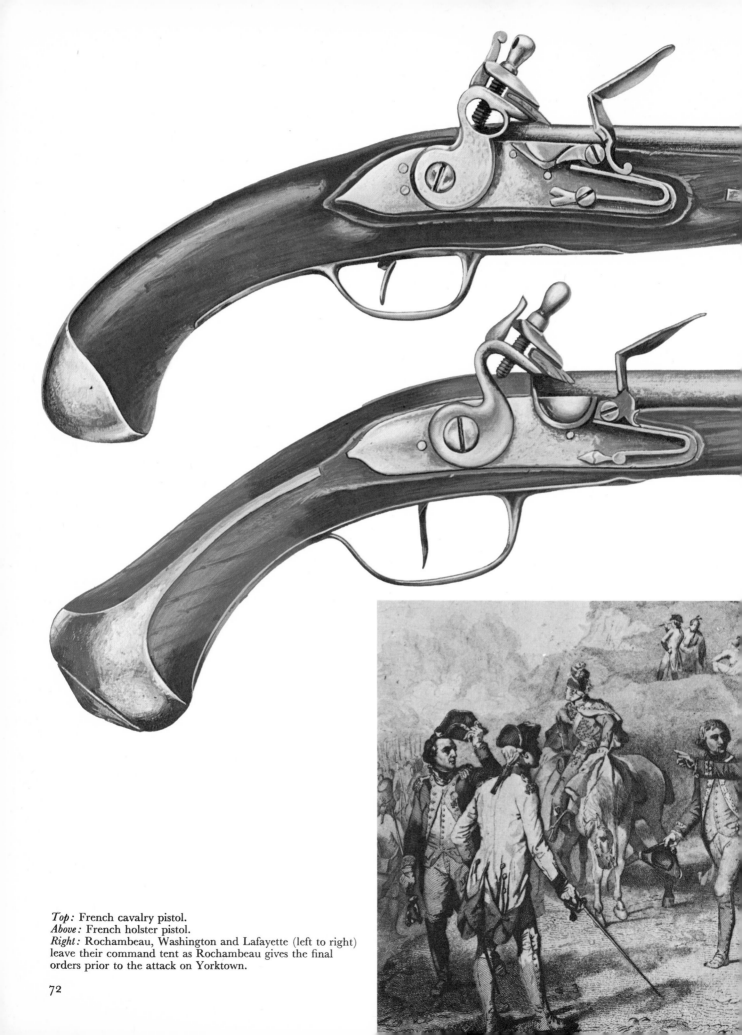

Top: French cavalry pistol.
Above: French holster pistol.
Right: Rochambeau, Washington and Lafayette (left to right) leave their command tent as Rochambeau gives the final orders prior to the attack on Yorktown.

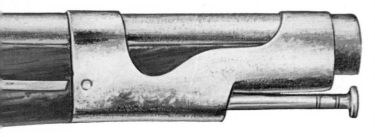

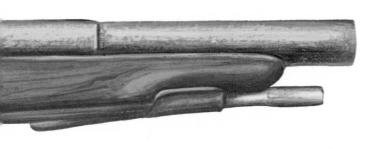

fire the issue ammunition. The ammunition question was less vital in the 1770s, when calibres varied from maker to maker and could generally be resolved by a suitable patch applied around the next lower calibre of bullet if need be. Holster pistols therefore tended to vary around .62 calibre, barrels usually being about fifteen inches. On the other hand, since they were made by civil gunsmiths to less exacting specifications than military weapons, they tended to be more graceful and were certainly lighter; a 15-inch holster pistol rarely turned the scales at more than two pounds. Once again the individuality of the gunsmith was allowed full rein, and ornamentation was the rule rather than the exception, examples often showing butt caps and side plates of solid silver, cast and engraved in intricate designs.

A class of pistol which achieved prominence during the War of Independence was the Scottish pistol; indeed, it is remarkable that some of the most famous pistols to survive the Revolution and to be exhibited today are Scottish. As the name implies, these pistols came from Scotland, but there is rather more to it than that; they are of unique design, instantly identifiable and impossible to confuse with any other contemporary type of pistol.

The first unusual feature of the Scottish pistols is that (with some rare exceptions of early date) they are entirely of metal instead of using the normal wooden butt and stock. The second feature which marks the type is the absence of any form of trigger guard and the forming of the trigger into a knob or ball. And the third special feature is the presence of a ball, usually matching the trigger, at the bottom of the butt; this is the handle of a vent-clearing pricker screwed into the butt so as to be readily available for reaming out the vent between pan and chamber should it become fouled with powder residue.

Although the Scottish pistol was all metal, its basic construction was similar to any other; the flat-sided stockbutt was a separate unit of brass or, more usually, wrought iron, with the barrel fitted carefully in. The locks were basically standard flintlocks, but the sear mechanism was a modification of the original Dutch Snaphaunce lock in which the sear moved laterally across the axis of the gun, holding a tail on the cock and being withdrawn into the lock body to release it. The Scots modified this by doing away with the tail on the cock and moving the sear to the front side of the cock.

The last notable feature about the Scottish pistol was the ornamentation and shape of the butt, formed usually into a heart, a lemon or some similar shape or, most often, terminating in a graceful pair of

Far left: American holster pistol.
Below: American cavalry pistol.

Previous page: Francis Marion leads his guerrilla forces across the Pedee River during the Carolina campaign.
Below: Death of de Kalb, the German commander working for the Americans, at the Battle of Camden, South Carolina, 16 August 1780. In this battle Cornwallis' forces overwhelmed the Continental Army under the command of Horatio Gates.

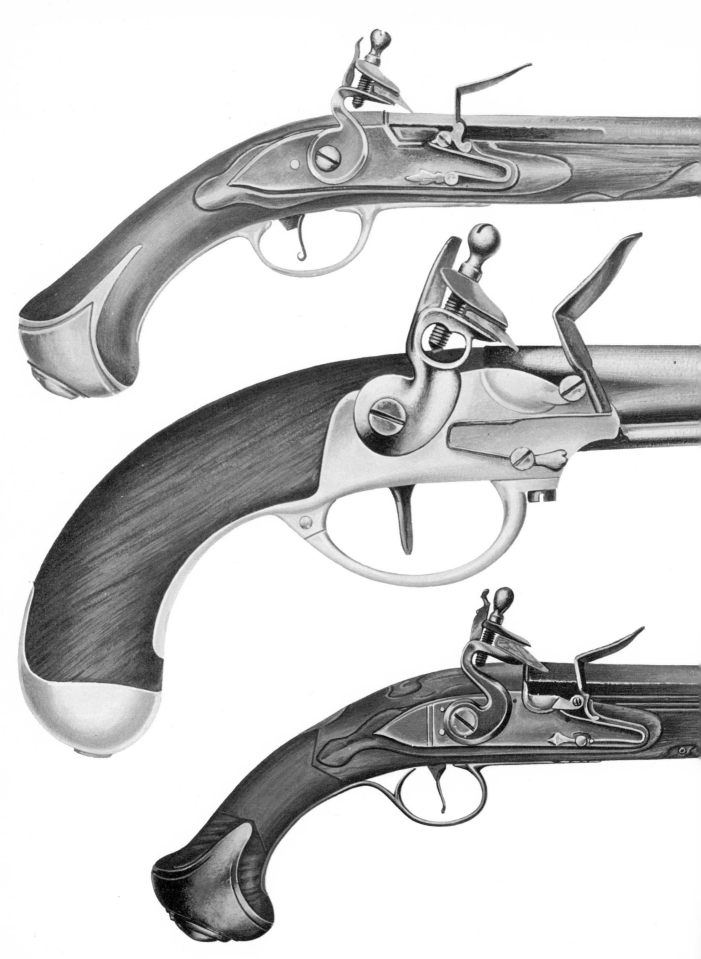

ram's horns between which the vent pricker was mounted.

The Scottish pistols were, in fact, all made in Scotland. I make the point in view of the 'Kentucky Rifle' discrepancy——and numerous makers became well-known in this specialist field. It is worth noting that while Scottish pistols are relatively common, Scottish muskets, exhibiting equally unique features, were also made but in relatively small numbers, and one authority has said that it is doubtful if more than a couple of dozen survive today. There is no such shortage of the pistols. Among the most famous of these were the pair carried by Major Pitcairn as saddle pistols at Lexington. On the return from Concorde to Boston, Pitcairn's horse was upset by a musket shot, Pitcairn was thrown off, and the horse bolted——with his pistols. The horse was subsequently caught by a party of Minutemen and the pistols were eventually presented to General Israel Putnam. They survived the war and today are in the Lexington Historical Society Museum, a fine pair of .55 calibre made by Murdock of Doune. Constructed entirely of iron, they are ornately engraved and bear Pitcairn's monogram and crest in medallions let into the butt. An unusual feature of these pistols is that although they are a matched pair, the locks are both on the right-hand side with belt hooks on the left. Most matched pairs of pistols were 'handed', that is, they had the locks on opposite sides so that the locks were outermost when the pistols were hooked into the belt and carried with the butts to the rear. It is also noteworthy that instead of using the belt hooks provided, Pitcairn was carrying them in saddle holsters, although when one considers their size—— the barrels are over a foot long——and their weight, it is understandable.

As to how the Scottish pistol got to America—— certainly they came with the Royal Highland Regiment well before the revolutionary days, and doubtless numbers were brought over by Scottish immigrants. And, as Pitcairn's example shows, many were purchased privately by officers of other regiments, since the all-metal construction made them exceptionally robust, a valuable attribute in a military weapon. There seems to be little doubt that they were highly prized; General George Washington carried one throughout the War of Independence, and on his death he left it to Lafayette.

The pistols available to the American forces represent weapons from practically every pistol-producing nation. Standard British military and commercial patterns predominated during the early days of the War, but once the Revolutionary movement

Top: German cavalry pistol.
Center: German holster pistol.
Above: French cavalry pistol.

Below : General George Washington's pair of silver mounted pistols, made by Hawkins of London.

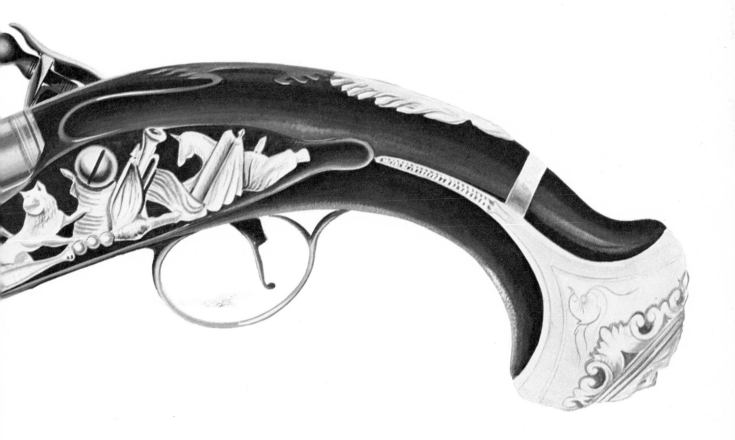

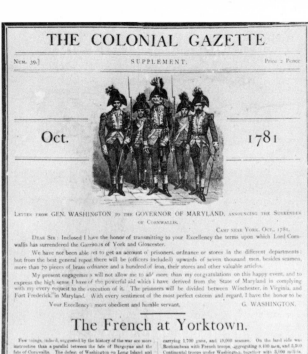

THE COLONIAL GAZETTE

Num. 39.]   SUPPLEMENT.   Price 2 Pence

Oct.   1781

LETTER FROM GEN. WASHINGTON TO THE GOVERNOR OF MARYLAND, ANNOUNCING THE SURRENDER OF CORNWALLIS.

CAMP NEAR YORK, OCT., 1781.

DEAR SIR : Inclosed I have the honor of transmitting to your Excellency the terms upon which Lord Cornwallis has surrendered the Garrisons of York and Gloucester.

We have not been able yet to get an account of prisoners, ordnance or stores in the different departments; but from the best general report there will be (officers included) upwards of seven thousand men, besides seamen, more than 70 pieces of brass ordnance and a hundred of iron, their stores and other valuable articles.

My present engagements will not allow me to add more than my congratulations on this happy event, and to express the high sense I have of the powerful aid which I have derived from the State of Maryland in complying with my every request to the execution of it. The prisoners will be divided between Winchester, in Virginia, and Fort Frederick, in Maryland. With every sentiment of the most perfect esteem and regard, I have the honor to be

Your Excellency's most obedient and humble servant, G. WASHINGTON.

The French at Yorktown.

Few things, indeed, suggested by the history of the war are more instructive than a parallel between the fate of Burgoyne and the fate of Cornwallis. The defeat of Washington on Long Island and the loss of New York had been attributed to the fact that his troops were raw militia. Yet it was mainly with just such men, and not with Continentals (as the regular soldiers of the united colonies were called), that the American commanders in northern New York overcame, in two successive battles, the well-disciplined and admirably appointed army of Burgoyne. This was the one brilliant military triumph achieved by either party in the whole course of the struggle; yet, strange to say, its most substantial fruit was the favorable effect on the negotiations which for two years Franklin had been pushing at the court of Versailles. It was not, however, until the beginning of the ensuing year that the French Ministry would even promise assistance to the colonies; and although their advances of money may from that time forward be said to have kept the continental army on its feet, they did not render effective military aid until the arrival of Count De Grasse in the Chesapeake, about the beginning of September, 1781.

The surrender of Cornwallis was the direct result of the advantages gained by De Grasse over Admiral Graves in the naval battle which took place at the mouth of Chesapeake Bay on September 5, 1781. For the first time during the war, the English failed to have a preponderance of naval strength in American waters, and for almost the first time an English Admiral, commanding a force not greatly inferior to his opponents, sailed pusillanimously away after an indecisive action, in which the French loss in killed and wounded was actually the greater. After this unexpected and inexcusable behaviour on the part of an English naval officer, the surrender of Cornwallis was clearly an obvious necessity. On one side there was the French fleet, comprising twenty four ships of the line

carrying 1,700 guns, and 19,000 seamen. On the land side was Rochambeau with French troops, aggregating 8,000 men, and 5,000 Continental troops under Washington, together with 3,000 militia, who were of less account. Against this military and naval force, Cornwallis had 7,500 men within the works of Yorktown, exclusive of 800 marines, disembarked from some English frigate which had lain in the river. Under these circumstances the surrender of the English force was plainly a mere question of time. It may be said, however, that the presence of the land force at a place where it could so happily co-operate with the French fleet, bears witness to great strategical ability, and it has been usual to give the credit of the combination to Washington. It is clear, however, that throughout the summer of 1781, the American commander had not seriously contemplated anything but a concerted attack on Sir Henry Clinton in New York. From the day, however, that De Grasse arrived in the Chesapeake, and visited the American and French commanders, that he would take his hopes no further northward, it required no great strategist to perceive that the land forces must operate in Virginia, if at all. It was from that moment the objective point of Washington and Rochambeau was palpably the force which Cornwallis, in obedience to Clinton's orders, had collected at Yorktown. Cornwallis, on his part, could not be counted, because he counted before, nor afterward, any Englishman have supposed it possible that an Admiral seeing the armament which Graves controlled would have acknowledged himself beaten on the sea by Frenchmen till half of his own were sunk.

In view of these facts, it behooves us in this great celebration at Yorktown, to render our French visitors the honors they deserve, for the event commemorated is more truly and emphatically a French than an American achievement.

Yours most truly

Cornwallis

Left: Item from the *Colonial Gazette* which headlined Washington's letter to the Governor of Maryland announcing Cornwallis' surrender.
Bottom: Autographed picture of Cornwallis, from an engraving by Ritchie.
Right: American holster pistol.

got under way supplies from Europe expanded the list. Dutch pistols were a common item, not only because they were purchased from Holland during the Revolution, but also due to their importation commercially during prewar days. Moreover, during the war, the Dutch turned out large numbers of pistols to fill contracts from Britain, France and from American emissaries. Specimen Dutch pistols range from .65 to .69 calibre and up to $3\frac{1}{4}$ pounds in weight, with barrels varying from 11 to 15 inches long.

The French pistols, which were eventually to become the American standard, came in a bewildering variety of designs. Standardization of French service pistols began with the Model of 1733; this had a part-octagonal barrel and an elliptical front sight. With a 12-inch .69 calibre barrel, it weighed about $2\frac{3}{4}$ pounds. This was then replaced by the Model of 1766, which is generally held to be the most common pistol in American hands during the latter part of the war. This model had a 9-inch .65 calibre barrel, weighed about $2\frac{1}{2}$ pounds, and is easily recognizable by the large barrel-retaining band and ramrod holder. The barrel is round, while the butt cap is severely plain and the whole weapon devoid of ornamentation, though having said this it should be added that models will occasionally be found with the half-octagonal barrel of the Model of 1733, since barrels on hand for

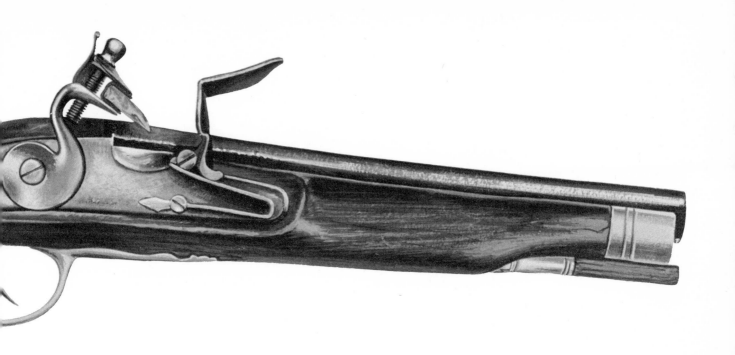

that weapon were shortened and used to build Model 1766 pistols.

Next came the Model of 1773; the only change from the Model of 1766 lay in the contour of the lock plate, which was rounded behind the cock instead of being flat. But this model was soon replaced by the Model of 1777 or Pistolet d'Arcon, a considerably simplified design attributed to one Honoré Blanc. This used a 7½-inch barrel of .69 calibre, and is noted for being one of the first military pistols to abandon the practice of stocking the muzzle. The tapered barrel has no support beneath, while the lock and trigger are carried in a cast brass housing which serves also as a ramrod holder. The simplicity, reliability and robustness of this model commended itself to the American forces, and it was the pattern selected to be copied in postwar years as the first United States Martial Pistol, the Model of 1799.

As with most armies, French officers usually provided themselves with commercial holster pistols, and quantities of these found their way to America. Generally speaking they were much the same as the English equivalents: barrels varying from six to nine inches, calibres from .58 to .69, and liberally ornamented.

In a similar fashion to their adoption of musket patterns, when the American army found it necessary to manufacture pistols, it derived its patterns from the various types available at the time. In addition, European pistols damaged in battle were salvaged and rebuilt in American workshops, taking on distinctly American properties in the process. Several specimens exist of identifiably British, German and French barrels fitted into plain wooden stocks, often without provision for a ramrod and with extremely simple furniture. A characteristic American feature was the use of a smooth butt cap with side-pieces, bearing no ornamentation at all. The locks and trigger guards are also of more utilitarian design than those originally associated with the barrels.

The advantage of rifled barrels being appreciated, it can be no surprise to discover that the hands which fashioned the American rifles also made pistols. These were obviously a more difficult and expensive proposition than a simple smoothbore, and because of this their numbers were relatively few, almost all of which became officers' weapons. Like the rifles they were beautifully made and finished, often with curly maple stocks and octagonal barrels. The pattern of various components——side plates, butt caps, fore-end caps——parallels the contemporary rifles, while their efficiency is attested to by the almost universal fitting of fore and rear sights, items rarely seen on the smoothbore pistols of the day.

Edged Weapons

The other class of hand weapon of the 18th century was, of course, the various edged weapons——swords, hangers, cutlasses and the like. By the time of the War of Independence the sword was no longer a standard article of apparel, but nevertheless it was a common enough property, and many of the swords which appeared in the War were of non-military origins.

The standard military sword was known as a 'hanger', since it was carried hanging from a cross-belt. Virtually all foot soldiers carried hangers until the rise of the bayonet in the early part of the 18th century, after which the hanger was restricted to use by NCOs. As befitted a weapon issued to the rank and

Far left: Five American hangers.
Below: Storming of the Redoubt at Yorktown.
Above: Redcoats charging the Minute Men at Bunker Hill, 17 June 1775.

file, the average hanger was a plain and robust article which could withstand the hurly-burly of campaigning, but even so, some of them managed to be graceful with it.

The standard English hangers——the design varied slightly over the years——used a single-edged blade of 24 to 30 inches long, with a hilt of wood, horn or cast brass and a brass guard and quillons, or cross-pieces. The blade was rarely entirely straight, usually having a slight reverse curve and a false edge at the tip. It should, perhaps, be pointed out that it was the intended use of the sword which dictated the shape of the blade. For offensive purposes——swinging and slashing——a curved single-edged blade was best. The curve increased the cutting power by reducing resistance, while the single-edged blade gave the desired rigidity for a cutting stroke. On the other hand, a defensive sword was one more suited to thrusting, in which case the blade was better straight and of a rigid triangular or square section. But, as is apparent from most specimens, military blades had to be a compromise between these two ideals, sufficiently curved to be a useful cutting weapon, but not so acutely curved and supple as to destroy their ability to be used as thrusting swords.

While regulations were fairly fluid, it was at least expected that any one regiment would have swords of a uniform pattern throughout, and Commanding Officers were allowed a wide discretion in the pattern they chose to adopt. As a result many English regiments had their sword hilts cast in brass and incorporating some motif peculiar to the regiment, either the regimental badge or some symbol forming part of the badge. While these brass hilts look extremely smart, they were not apparently highly regarded by the soldiers; in the first place they were difficult to keep clean in barracks, and in the second place they were difficult to handle in combat, since the polished brass hilt gave a poor grip when the wielder's hand was wet with sweat or blood. It is notable that naval cutlasses, much more likely to be used than an infantryman's sword, rarely used brass hilts; a less slippery material was favored.

While English regiments were content with their hangers, the Scottish regiments would have none of them, and retained their traditional basket-hilt broadsword, commonly, but not accurately, called the 'Claymore'. These swords had a wooden hilt bound with wire to give a firm grip, a double-edged blade, and the characteristic and ornate 'basket' guard of pierced iron. The guard design was generally a stylized floral pattern, and, again, some effort was made to achieve a uniform pattern throughout a

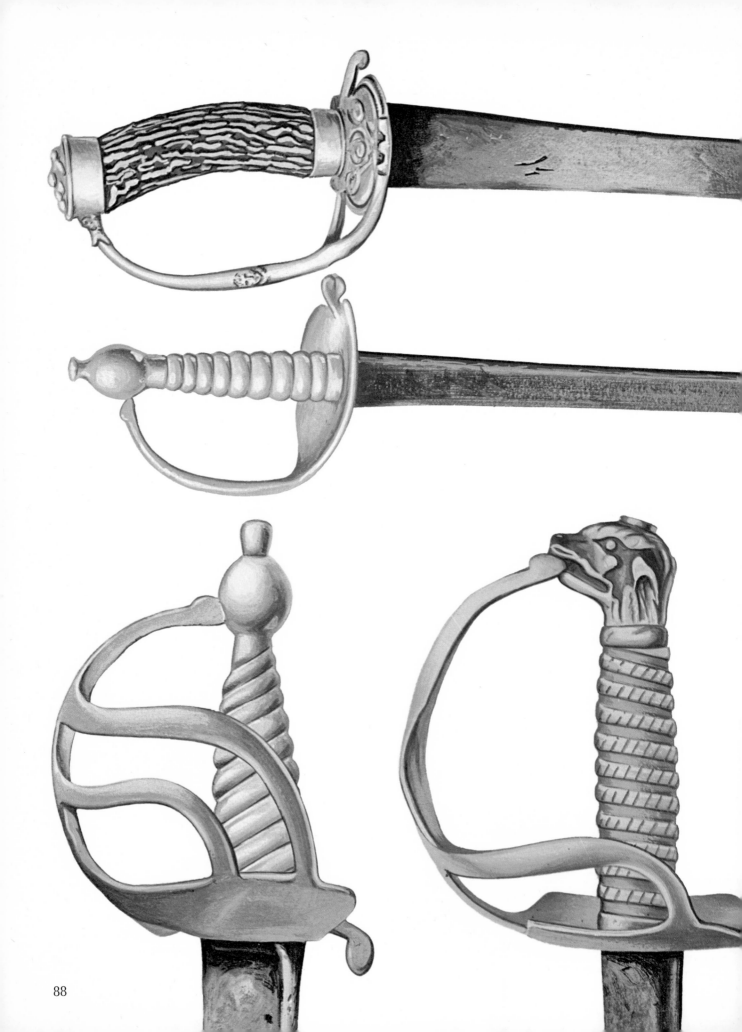

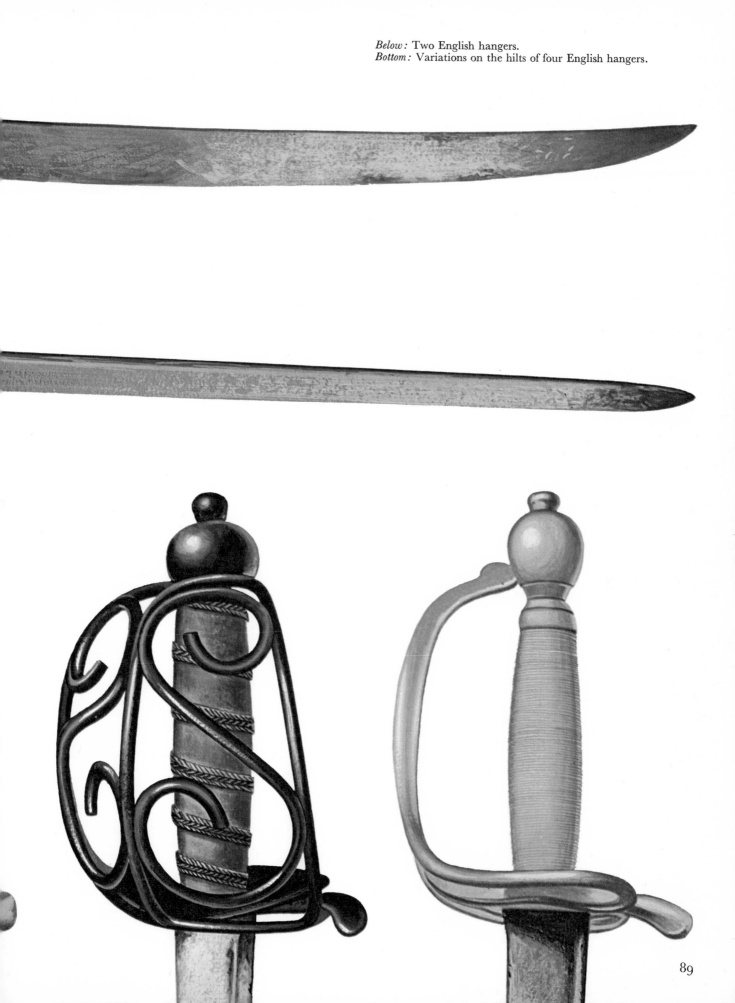

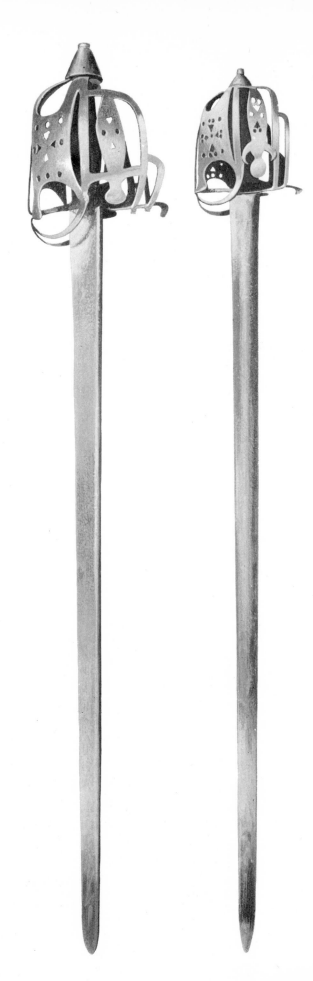

regiment. An exception to the general description was the single-edged basket-hilt sword; these were certainly used by the 42nd of Foot and possibly by other Scottish regiments, but they were less common than the double-edged variety.

As with other weapons, the swords carried by officers were generally of a better quality than those issued to the rank and file. Most officers provided their own swords, and the preferred type was of the class generally called 'small swords'. These were lighter than hangers and were intended for use by gentlemen schooled in the art of fencing, people who could use a sword's capabilities to the full. Blades were generally straight and of small section, intended for thrust-and-parry tactics rather than the full-blooded swinging of a hanger or broadsword. A common pattern of blade, especially on the Continent, was the *colichemarde* blade; the word is a French corruption of Königsmark where the design originated, and the blade is formed in two widths. From the hilt, for about nine inches or approximately a third of the blade's length, it is wide and with two blunt edges; then it narrows abruptly to a thinner double-edged section, tapering to a slender point. This form of construction was popular because it gave strength to the blade near the hilt, where it was needed to turn an opponent's blade, while retaining lightness at the tip, and by adjusting the length of the wider section during manufacture, the sword could be balanced very precisely without sacrificing strength or length.

Another pattern of sword sometimes favored by officers was of the class known as 'hunting swords'. As a rule these can be distinguished by the absence of any form of knuckle guard, since they were intended either as ornament or, as the name implies, as workaday swords for use when hunting, and there was no requirement to protect the sword hand against an enemy's blade. In order to prevent loss, the tip of the hilt——the pommel——was frequently connected to the quillons by a loop of fine chain.

The last type of sword deserving recognition is that of the mounted trooper——the sabre. The cavalry

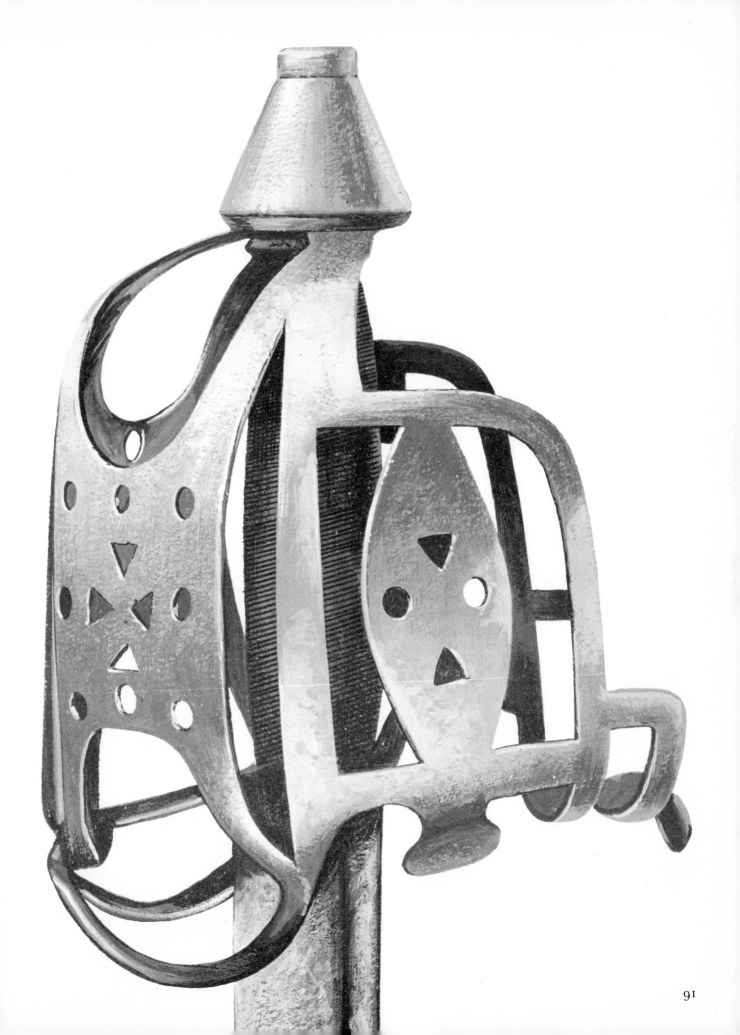

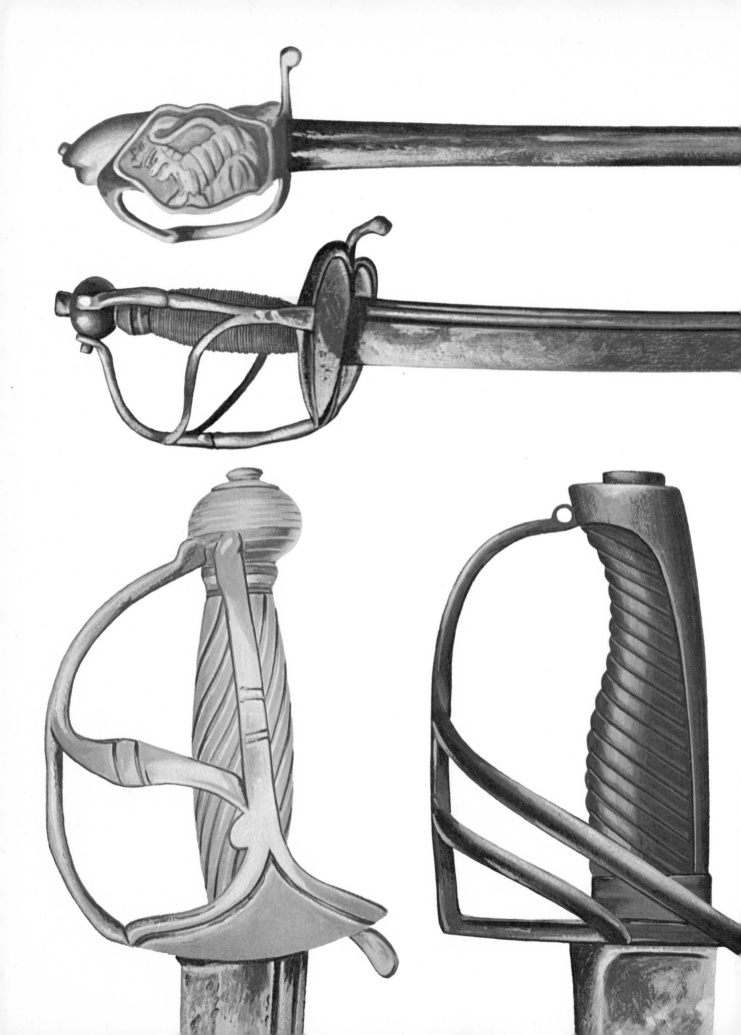

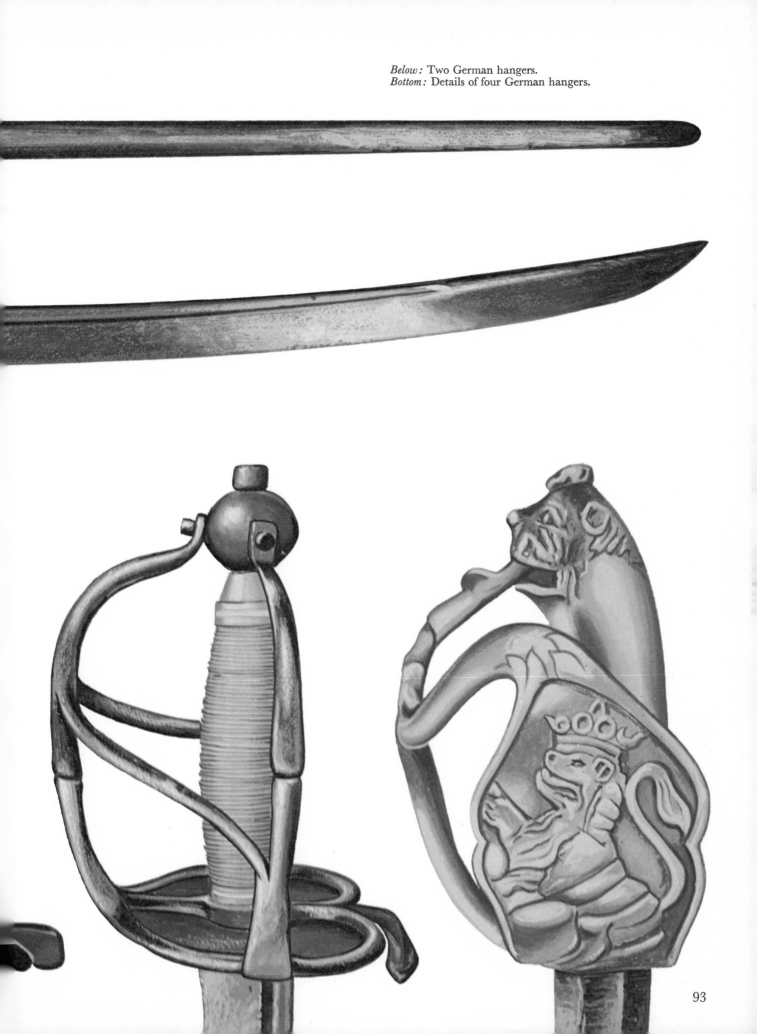

Previous page: Colonel William Washington at the Battle of Cowpens, 17 January 1781. In this battle Banastre Tarleton's British forces were dessimated by the Americans under Daniel Morgan.
Right: American horseman sabres.
Below right: English horseman sabres.

sword had undergone a change at the end of the 17th century. Prior to this the cavalry tactic was solely the charge, with the sword held straight out at arms length to give point and act as a thrusting weapon. Then came the Hussars, Hungarian cavalry wielding curved swords to cut and slash their way through the opposition, and within a few years every army in Europe had formed Hussar regiments and adopted the curved sabre throughout their cavalry. The degree of curvature was a matter for some debate and no standard ever became accepted internationally; some sabres curved continuously from the hilt, while others have a lesser degree of curvature allied to a straight section near the hilt. Indeed, some English cavalry sabres were entirely straight. The only definite feature of cavalry swords was that they were invariably longer and heavier than those issued to foot soldiers, reflecting their carriage on the horse accoutrements rather than on the person and the need for extra weight to add to the already considerable shock effect of being wielded from horseback.

The bayonet of Revolutionary days was a simple weapon which admitted of little variety in design. To appreciate the form taken by the bayonet of the day it is necessary first to appreciate exactly what it was intended for. While the popular picture is of opposing soldiers virtually fencing with musket and bayonet, this was a secondary use. Primarily the bayonet was an anti-cavalry **defense** and not an anti-personnel offensive weapon. On receiving the order 'Prepare to Resist Cavalry' the troops knelt in two ranks 'bringing the firelock in front of the right knee, the lock turned uppermost, the right hand grasping the small of the butt, holding the firelock firm with the left hand . . . the muzzle of the firelock slanting upwards so that the point of the bayonet will be about the height of a horse's nose. . . .' The remaining troops formed two standing ranks behind this prickly fence and as the cavalry approached, opened fire. If necessary the kneeling ranks quickly came to the 'Present', fired, and resumed the 'resist' position. After the volley the rear ranks also knelt so that four rows of bayonets 'about

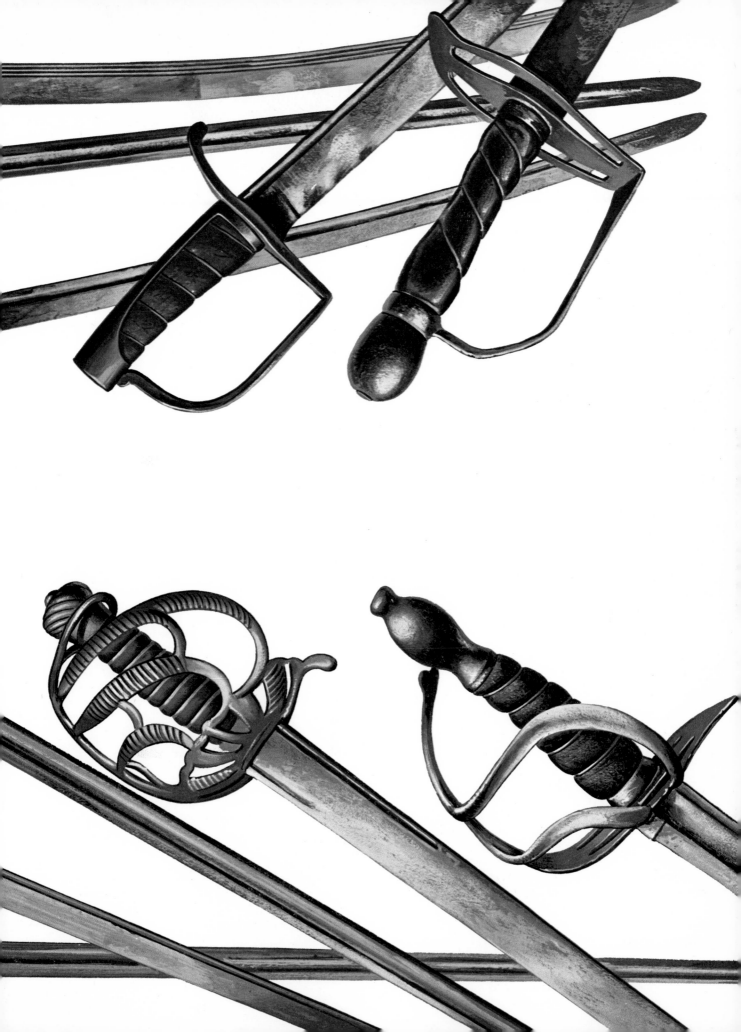

the height of a horse's nose' were firmly anchored and ready to disembowel any horse which tried to leap over.

Nevertheless, there were occasions when the bayonet came into its own as a hand-to-hand weapon. One notable affray was at Princeton when the 17th of Foot (The Leicestershire Regiment) were cut off. Discarding their packs to give themselves greater freedom of movement, they proceeded to cut their way out using the bayonet. In this sort of situation the disciplined and practised regular was at a considerable advantage; effective use of a musket and bayonet——six and a half feet long and weighing twelve or thirteen pounds—— demanded training and long practice.

The normal bayonet of the day, of any nation, was in consequence a fairly standardized article. All bayonets were, at this time, socket bayonets; that is, they terminated in a hollow socket which fitted more

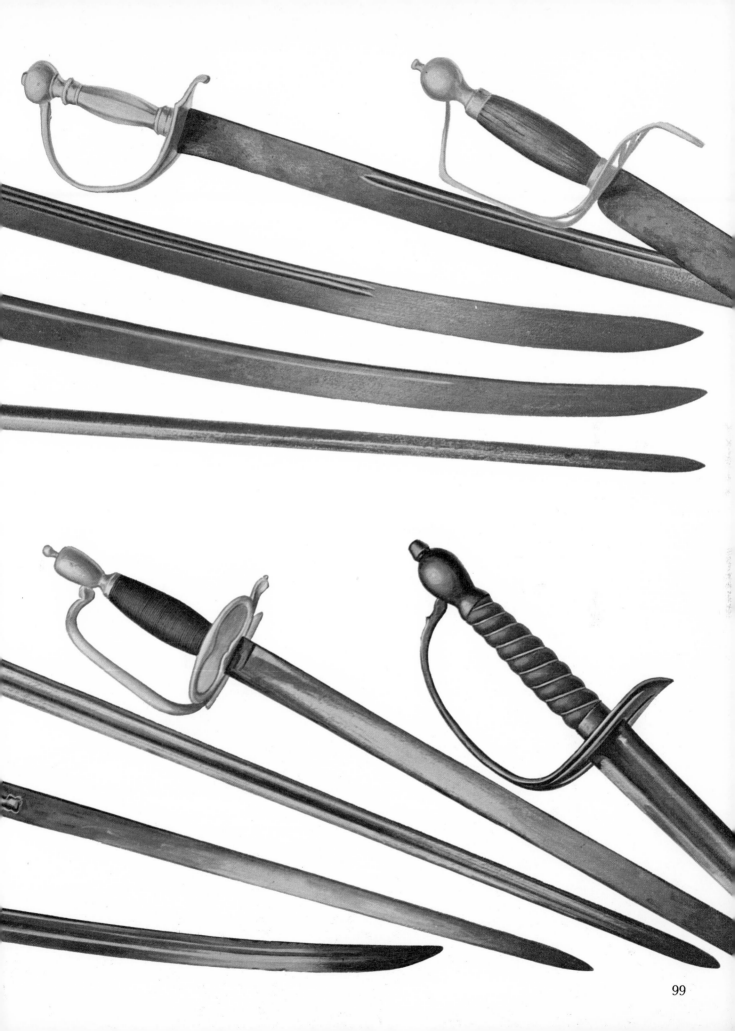

Previous page: The death of General Montgomery on New Year's Eve 1775 marked the end of American hopes to capture Canada. The siege of Quebec undertaken by Benedict Arnold and Richard Montgomery was thwarted by the British in the fortress during a blinding snowstorm.
Far right: George Washington's swords.
Below right: American halberds.
Bottom: Arrival of the French troops at Newport, Rhode Island, from a German engraving. General Rochambeau was able to help Washington tie down British forces in New York City once the successful landing had been made.

or less snugly over the muzzle of the musket. A slot cut in the socket engaged with the foresight so that the bayonet was slipped on to the muzzle and then given a half turn to bring the foresight into a recess in the slot, preventing the bayonet from being pulled from the musket. This resulted in the bayonet being positioned at the side of the weapon, instead of, as today, beneath the muzzle.

The bayonet blade originally was based on the contemporary sword blade, a wide and flat double-edged style, but this meant a somewhat fragile and supple blade, not good for resisting a charging horse, and by the late 18th century the normal blade contour was a more or less flattened triangle, the edges sharpened and the centre thickened to give maximum strength.

The Brown Bess bayonet had a 17-inch blade and a four-inch socket. The usual French bayonet had a 14-inch blade and was an improvement on the British design, in that the socket carried a locking ring which could be tightened against the foresight of the musket when the bayonet was fixed in order to give a more secure fitting than the British pattern which relied entirely on friction. The American bayonets were largely copies of either the British or French designs, though in the latter case they rarely bothered with the locking ring. Moreover they were less standardized than the foreign designs, since they were frequently hand made to measure for a specific weapon and were not interchangeable.

Certain other weapons deserve mention, though they were less offensive weapons than badges of authority. Officers normally carried a 'spontoon' in addition to their sword. The spontoon was a form of pike, a pole with an ornamental spearhead and cross-pieces which, in the original form, were supposed to prevent over-penetration when thrust into an enemy. But by 1775 the spontoon's head had moved away from the spartan simplicity of a utilitarian blade on a pole and had blossomed forth with floral engravings on the blade, decorative finials on the cross-piece and various other additions and refinements. While the

Right: The siege of Charleston, South Carolina. After the British took the port in 1779, Admiral d'Estaing tried unsuccessfully to recapture it in 1780. Charleston was the largest port in the South and its retention was vital to the maintenance of British supplies to Cornwallis during his Carolina campaigns.
Below: English infantry and artillery hall swords.

spontoon was still carried on formal parades, it was not, by this time, held in much regard on the battle-field, the sword and fusil being more commonly carried by officers.

Sergeants carried a halberd as their mark of authority. This was also a pole weapon, somewhat more utilitarian, with the head formed into an axe-blade surmounted by a spearhead. The spearhead could doubtless still be used as a thrusting weapon, but the axe portion had degenerated into a stylized curved shape of little practical worth. In fact contemporary records suggest that the principal function of the halberd, at least in the British Army, was to be tied together in threes to form an extemporized 'triangle' for flogging malefactors.

Although it can hardly be classed as a military weapon, a standard item of equipment which practically every soldier on the American continent carried was a tomahawk or hatchet, slung from the belt. At least, it was not issued as a weapon, but sufficient evidence exists to show that it frequently became one in the heat of the moment. These were, of course, commercial or 'trade' items bought either individually or under contract arrangements by a regiment, and there were no sealed patterns or regulation standard models.

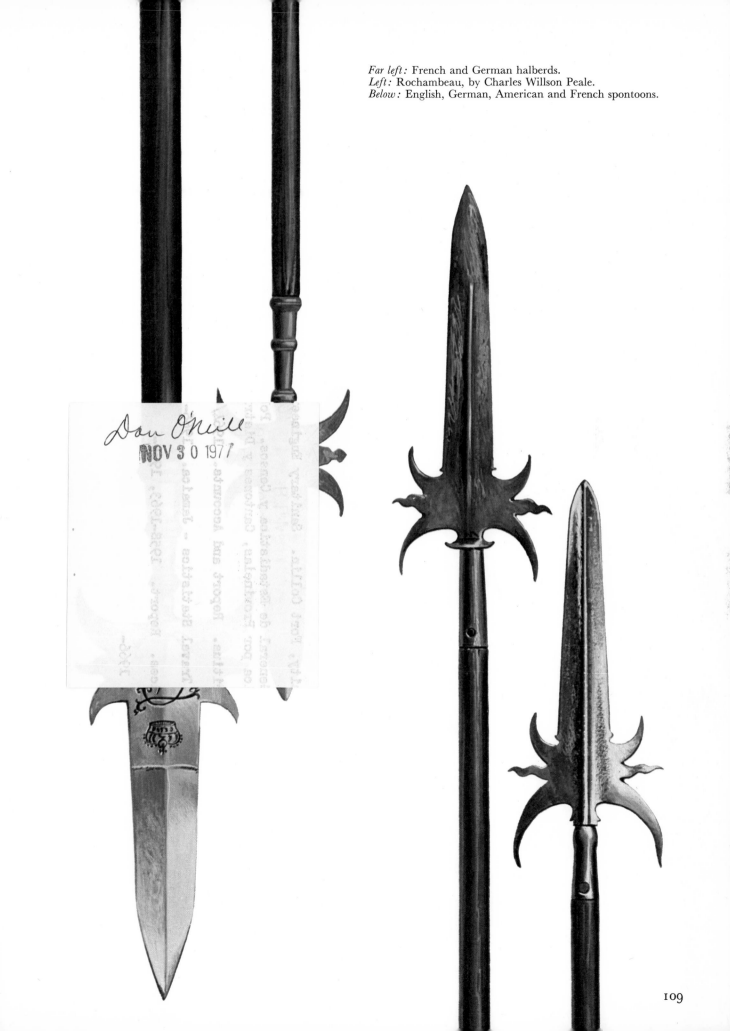

Far left: French and German halberds.
Left: Rochambeau, by Charles Willson Peale.
Below: English, German, American and French spontoons.

Artillery

The artillery of the War of Independence was without exception the standard smooth-bore muzzle-loading cannon which had seen little change in the previous two hundred years and which was destined to serve, in places, for another century. By this time most features of design had been settled; the cannon was cast of iron or bronze; it was loaded with a prepared cartridge of paper or cloth containing gunpowder, followed by a spherical projectile; it was fired by igniting a goose-quill tube of quickmatch inserted into the vent; and when it fired, it leaped back due to the recoil and had to be manhandled back into the firing position after being reloaded.

Three types of ordnance were to be found; the gun, the howitzer and the mortar. The gun was long in relation to its calibre and fired at as high a velocity as could be obtained at targets within sight—— direct shooting with a relatively flat trajectory. The howitzer was shorter barrelled, fired at a lower velocity and at a higher angle of elevation to pitch the projectile over intervening obstacles; the projectile

Left: English 6-pdr. cannon.
Above: Alexander Hamilton in the uniform of an officer of the
New York Artillery Company, circa 1776. Hamilton became
the first Secretary of the Treasury in Washington's cabinet of
1789 after the Constitution was formed.

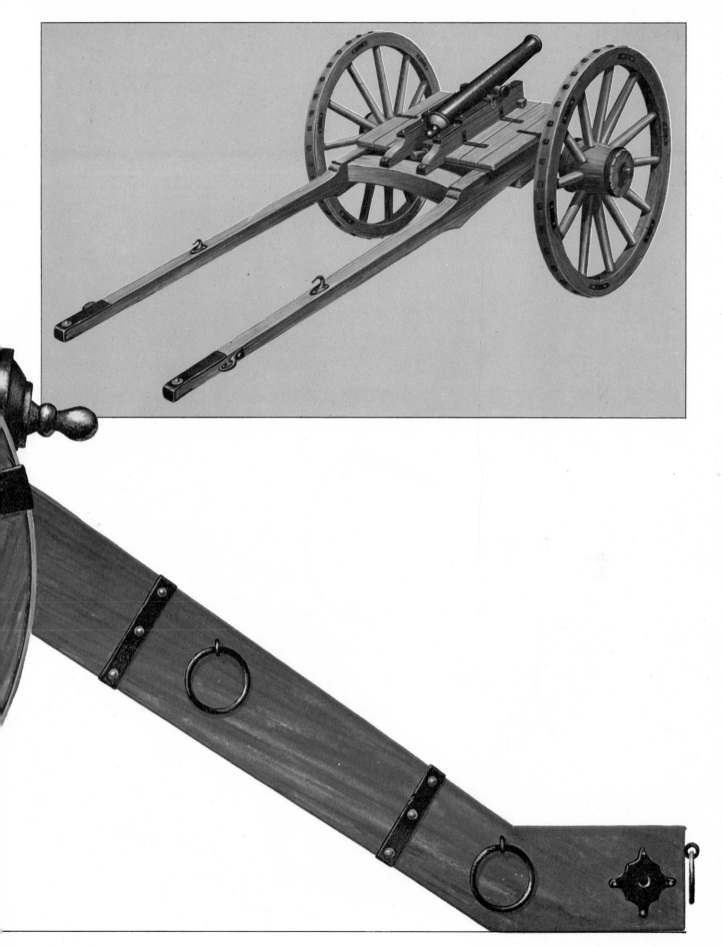

was generally a powder-filled shell. The mortar, which also fired an explosive projectile, was a short stumpy weapon which launched its shell at high angles so as to pass high into the air, pass over fortifications and breastworks, and drop steeply on to its target.

Guns and howitzers were alike mounted on the simple carriages of the day, either the block trail carriage or the flask carriage. These were little more than an axle-tree with two wheels, upon which was laid one or two baulks of timber, shaped at the rear to lie upon the ground and formed at the front into cheek-pieces to hold the cannon trunnions. Block trails had the trail unit formed of a single piece of timber, a form of construction adequate for the lighter guns, while flask trails had the trail made of two side-pieces with the gun slung between them, allowing heavier cannon to be mounted. Very light guns could be found on 'galloper' carriages, the

cannon being fixed to a platform above the axle and the trails actually shaped to form shafts, between which the horse could be harnessed to move the gun. Larger weapons required a two-wheeled 'limber' to be run beneath the end of the trail, thus converting the gun into a four-wheeled load. The limber had a single wagon tongue attached to the front, and a team of horses, mules or oxen could be harnessed in the usual fashion.

Sighting the cannon was done by a notch on the muzzle swell and a similar notch on the base ring, and elevation was given either by rule of thumb, the gunner's eye, or, more formally, by use of the gunner's quadrant and plumb-bob. Elevation was applied to the gun by wooden 'quoins' or wedges, forced beneath the breech, though by this time some guns were fitted with screw elevating mechanisms. This had been introduced in the middle of the previous century, but it was still regarded as a luxurious refinement

Right: Lafayette, by Charles Willson Peale.
Below: French mortar.

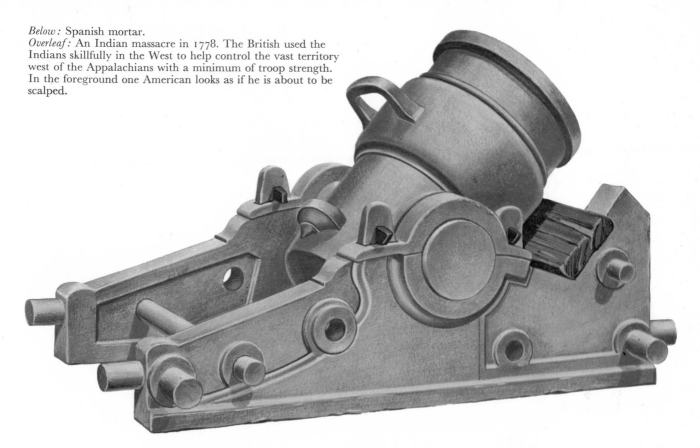

and it was far from being a standard fitment. In order to retain the quoins in place, guns were so cast as to have 'preponderance'; the breech section behind the trunnions was some hundred pounds or so heavier than the muzzle section, so that the gun always tended to rest firmly against the elevating quoin.

The ammunition limber, a small specialized cart to carry the gun's ready-use ammunition supply, had been developed during the Seven Years War, some fifteen years before the Revolution, but it appears not to have gained much acceptance by 1775 and there are no reports of their use in America. The ready-use supply was provided by small boxes attached to the axle tree or hung between the side members of the gun trail for traveling and unstrapped and laid on the ground before opening fire. These boxes carried only a handful of rounds sufficient to allow a rapid response from the gun on being confronted with a quick call to action; it was necessary for the ammunition wagons to be brought up and unloaded before sustained fire could be brought to bear.

Artillery tactics were just about non-existent at this time; tactics imply movement, and movement was an involved business with the guns of the day. Their speed was the speed of the gunners walking alongside, and once deployed in battle there could be no question of rapid re-deployment to take advantage of a sudden enemy move. Fortunately the American battles were relatively small affairs by European standard, and once the guns were positioned they could generally command the more important sectors of the field without having to redeploy.

The normal method of employing field artillery at that time was to form all the available guns into a 'Grand Battery' and plant this squarely in the centre of the line. An alternative sometimes followed was to place individual companies at intervals between the infantry battalions. The guns could then open the battle by briskly bombarding the enemy infantry or their guns; it was a question of gambling. If you chose to open fire on the enemy infantry, while his guns opened fire on your artillery, then there was a very good chance that your guns would suffer considerably. On the other hand, if you chose to batter his guns while he fired at your infantry, you were liable to be stigmatized as an idiot by the suffering foot-soldiers. And if both batteries hammered at each other, they were liable to be accused of fighting a private war, and how about doing something useful like shooting at the enemy infantry? Artillery command was no sinecure.

Due to the limited sphere of influence of the round shot of the day, a favored artillery gambit was to site the guns to the flank of the intended battlefield. In this way, it was hoped, the line formation of the

Top: View of Yorktown from the York River, a sketch drawn by a British officer about 1754.
Above: An English 18-pdr. cannon, which was used to defend Yorktown in 1781.

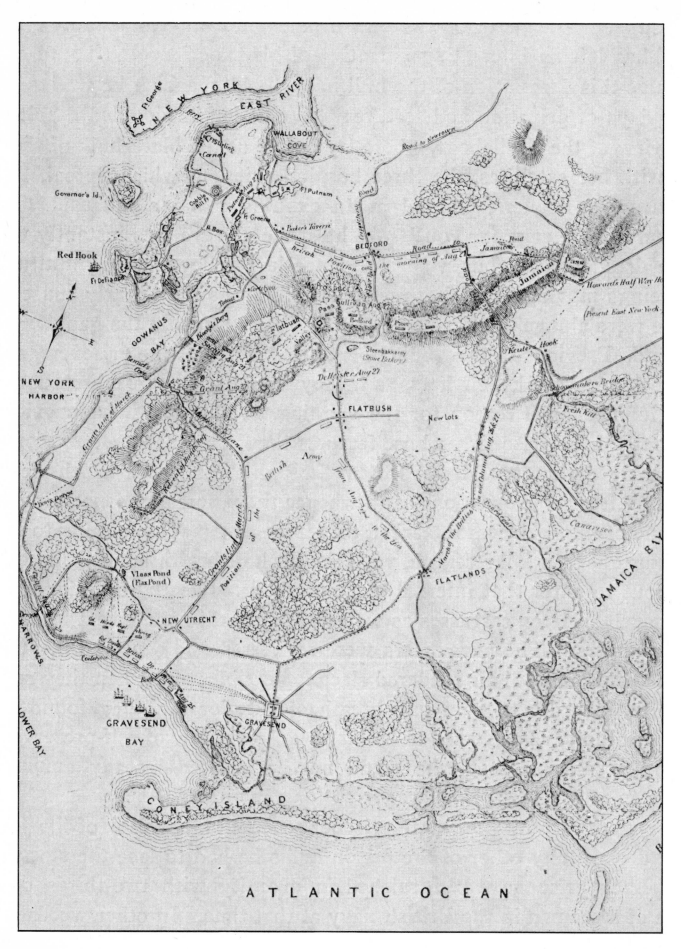

enemy would coincide sooner or later with the line of fire of the guns, and great execution would be done when the enemy were thus 'taken in enfilade'. The mass and velocity of a 32-pounder cannonball——something in the order of 200 foot-tons——could do considerable damage before being absorbed or dispersed. There is a case on record of 42 men being mown down like ninepins by a single ball which took their line in enfilade.

Once battle had been joined in earnest and the infantry began to advance, the guns were at a disadvantage. They could not move with the advance, and they were unable to go in firing once they were masked by the movement of their own troops. Techniques of indirect fire, over the heads of their own infantry into the ranks of the enemy, were some years in the future. The subsequent activities of the guns depended on the course of the infantry battle; the guns of the victors were limbered up and moved on, while those of the vanquished were overrun by the enemy advance, since they could rarely be brought out of action quickly enough to save them from capture. Guns changed hands frequently during a campaign, and the loss of guns was considered a normal hazard of battle and did not carry the stigma it was to gain a few years later when lighter ordnance and better horse teams made the saving of guns a more likely proposition.

Another factor which added to the difficulty was that while the guns were actually operated in battle by soldiers, they were transported by civilian teamsters and carters working on contract. And as they were not slow to point out, their terms of reference dealt solely with moving guns to and from the scene of action, and certainly not risking their lives under enemy fire. As a result, the first people to make themselves scarce when the bullets began to fly were the artillery teamsters, taking their precious horses with them, and if the hard-pressed gunners needed to move their guns there was no means of doing so other than manpower.

This vexed problem of civilian teamsters was one which afflicted every army of the age, since owners of armies were reluctant to foot the bill, in peacetime, for a host of ineffectives. Soldiers could be raised rapidly when the need arose, and dispersed equally rapidly when the war was over, and it seemed logical to acquire transport facilities the same way. Eventually the folly of this system was appreciated, and as the century drew to its close more and more armies began to reorganize their artillery to do away with the contractor and bring the entire force into uniform and under military control and discipline.

During the Revolution both the British and American artillery relied upon contract draught for their movement, but the British had the worst of it. With a limited amount of horseflesh available, and with contractors reluctant to ally themselves with the Redcoats, much of the transportation capacity had to be shipped across the Atlantic. On the other hand the American teamsters, while distinct from the Army, still had a fellow-feeling for 'their' soldiers and were more inclined to risk their lives and those of their horses for the cause of the Revolution.

British artillery used a mixed bag of both bronze and iron ordnance interchangeably, and within each calibre group there were generally a number of variant models. This was simply due to the relative indestructability of the muzzle-loading cannon; even if a new pattern were introduced it did not necessarily mean that all the earlier models were made redundant. They continued in service, perhaps being relegated to stations of lesser importance. Thus, in the case of the six-pounder gun (nominal 3.66 inch calibre) there were no less than fifteen variations in service; seven iron guns ranging from a six-foot of $16\frac{1}{2}$ hundredweight to a nine-foot of 24 hundredweight; seven bronze guns, from a five-foot of $5\frac{1}{2}$ hundredweight to an eight-foot of $19\frac{1}{4}$ hundredweight; and a carronade, two feet nine inches long weighing $4\frac{3}{4}$ hundredweight. Because of this complexity, it is necessary to specify the length and weight of any British gun in order to distinguish it from others of similar calibre.

The question of whether a gun was of bronze or

Far left: Cannon on the battlefield of Yorktown which can still be seen by visitors to the site.
Left: At Concord Bridge, by N. C. Wyeth. The Minute Men tried to block the British retreat from Lexington in 1775.
Below: English howitzer.

iron was of more than academic interest to the gunner, since it governed the weapon's power. Generally speaking iron guns were stronger and therefore they were able to fire heavier charges; the regulation called for a powder charge of one-third the weight of the round shot for the gun. Bronze guns, on the other hand, were restricted to a charge of only one-quarter of the shot weight. As a result iron guns could usually be expected to reach to a greater range than their equivalent in bronze; an iron six-pounder could range to 1500 yards, while a bronze six-pounder could only manage 1200 yards. Bronze guns did have the advantage that they were generally a good deal lighter than their iron equivalents of the same length, so that bronze guns were preferred for campaigning, even though the range was less, since they could be moved more easily. Another reason for retaining bronze ordnance was that when, eventually, the gun was so worn as to be unserviceable, it could be melted down and recast; an iron gun could only be scrapped.

The ranges quoted above are from a contemporary document which specifies the elevation of the gun to produce these ranges as four degrees; four degrees is not very much elevation, and it would be reasonable to assume that by increasing the elevation more range would have been achieved. Theoretically this is quite true, but it was never put into practice for a number of reasons. In the first place a greater elevation at the gun meant a correspondingly steeper angle of arrival at the target, and a steeply-descending cannon ball

simply buried itself in the ground. A ball fired at a lesser elevation arrived at a flatter angle, was dangerous to standing troops for a greater distance at the end of its flight, and then ricocheted and skipped across the ground haphazardly, making the enemy step very lively in all sorts of unpredictable directions.

A second point was that the standard simple design of gun carriage would not admit of much elevation being given to the gun barrel, nor was it engineered to resist recoil in a downward direction; fire at high angles would, therefore, have demanded a fresh approach to carriage design where powerful guns were involved. Howitzers, firing lesser charges, were less of a problem, and mortars used an entirely different pattern of carriage.

Finally came the simple fact that after about a thousand yards it became almost impossible to distinguish the strike of the shot with the naked eye or even with the assistance of the 'spy-glass' type of telescope of the day. There was, therefore, little incentive to launch cannonballs to long ranges when it would be impossible to determine their effect or accuracy.

The standard British guns in service in 1776 were as shown overleaf.

It should be noted that the calibres given above are nominal; the actual calibre varied between different models of the same gun, depending largely upon the current views on the question of windage. Moreover, as will be seen, the calibre of a given gun varied depending upon whether it was bronze or iron.

The howitzer began life as a gun intended to fire powder-filled explosive shells. This meant a generous calibre in order to get the best effect from the biggest shells, but it also meant that the propelling charge had to be reduced, to about one-ninth of the shell weight, in order not to place too great a strain on the hollow projectile. Since the small charge was quickly burned there was no need for a long barrel, and the howitzer therefore settled down to being a large-

calibre gun with a short barrel——about five to seven times the calibre was the accepted figure, as against 15–25 times for a normal gun.

The advantages of dropping the explosive shell over obstacles was introduced after the howitzer had entered service, and the design was soon modified to allow more elevation to the barrel to obtain plunging fire. Due to the short barrel and light charge this did not introduce any complications in the way of carriage design, although it must be stressed that in the 18th century an elevation of twenty degrees was considered high for a howitzer. It should also be added that although the elevation was increased over that of the contemporary gun, this was offset by the lower charge, and the howitzer never achieved greater ranges than guns of equivalent calibre.

The third class of ordnance, the mortars, also

Below: Types of shot. Left to right: Canister, grape, bar, chain, jointed bar, expanding bar, and round.

displayed a variety of types. At the time of the War of Independence there were nine different Land Service and four Sea Service Mortars in the British inventory, ranging from 4.4 inches to 13 inches in calibre and of bronze or iron. A peculiarity of the mortar's design was the 'chambering'——the boring of the powder chamber to a smaller diameter than the bore. Thus when loaded the shell rested on the lower edge of the bore with the powder charge in the chamber beneath it. Without this chambering the weight of the shell would have rested entirely on the powder, compressing the charge and making it difficult to ignite efficiently. Moreover, a chambered mortar meant that the ratio of air space to powder was constant from shot to shot, which led to regularity of ballistics and hence to a remarkable degree of consistency in shooting.

The barrels of mortars were never more than three calibres long and, in the case of large iron mortars, sometimes as short as one calibre. The charge was variable; no amount of research has yet managed to unearth an unequivocal statement of the maximum amount allowed, and it seems to have been largely left to the gunner's experience and wisdom. But the whole concept of range determination changed when mortars were used: instead of having a fixed charge and varying the elevation of the piece to pitch the projectile to the desired range, the mortar used a fixed elevation——45 degrees——and varied the charge in order to alter the range.

Due to the fixed elevation the construction of a carriage suitable for a mortar resolved itself into a very simple design; little more than a stout baulk of timber into which a recess was cut to take the breech

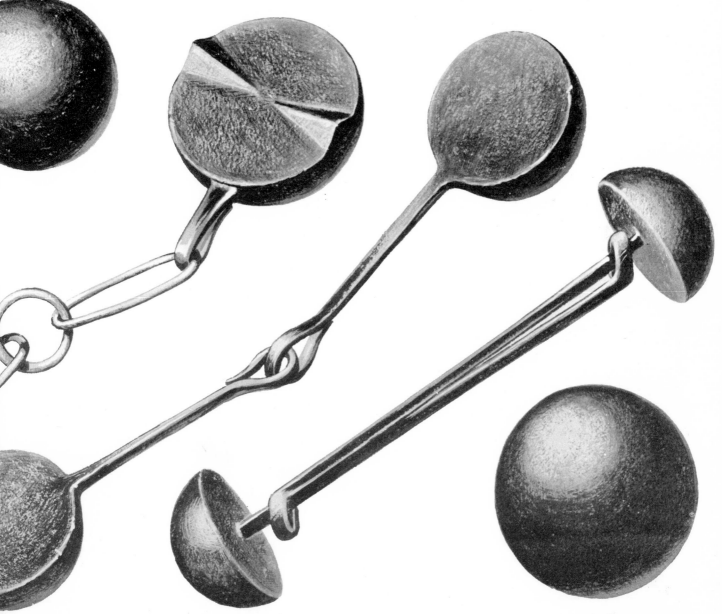

end of the piece and hold it at 45 degrees. Trunnions were always cast on the rear end of the mortar, but their principal role was that of spreading the recoil blow over a greater area of the baseplate rather than allowing for any movement of the piece in elevation. Sighting was done by scribing or painting a line down the top surface of the mortar barrel to coincide with the axis of the bore; this was aligned with the target by the gunner standing behind and holding a plumb-line in his hand. He sighted so that he saw the target on the far side of the plumb-line and had the axis line of the mortar barrel also in alignment with his plumb-line. This showed that the mortar was pointing at the target and, more important, that it was truly upright and not canted over to one side or another.

The standard mortars began with the 4.4 inch (actually called the 'Four and two-fifths inch') Coehorn Mortar, named after Baron de Coehorn who had been Director of Artillery of the Dutch Army in the 17th century and who had been responsible for the introduction of this design. Only 13¼ inches long, and weighing 84 lbs, the Coehorn could throw an 8½ lb shell to 800 yards range: it may have looked like a toy, but it was a useful weapon, since it could be rapidly moved and emplaced by two or three men.

The 'Royal' mortar——the origins of the title are unknown——was 5.4 inches calibre, 16½ inches long and weighed one hundredweight——112 pounds.

Below: English ammunition wagon.

Firing a sixteen pound shell to 1000 yards it too was a useful combination of firepower and weight.

The larger mortars came in two classes——Land or Sea Service——and were either of bronze or iron. Land Service mortars were lighter than their equivalent calibre of Sea Service mortar, since they had to be manhandled on and off carts and into position, whereas the Sea Service mortars were installed in 'bomb ketches' and needed no manhandling. The different varieties are tabulated opposite.

An odd class of mortar which was still in service at this time, though never shown on returns of ordnance or on inventories, was the 'Stone Mortar'. These were frequently of local or unofficial manufacture, followed no sealed pattern, and came in any and every calibre up to and including thirteen inch. They took their name from their ammunition; sacks or baskets of stones and scrap metal, fired entirely for their nuisance value. The maximum range was some four or five hundred yards at the best of times, and they were generally used during sieges in order to make life unpleasant for the occupants of the attacking trenches. Small calibres of stone mortar could also be used to throw the primitive hand grenades of the day, an interesting forerunner of the trench mortar, but one which saw limited employment.

The American Artillery came into being as a result of the existence of a small number of volunteer artillery companies in the Colonies. When the call

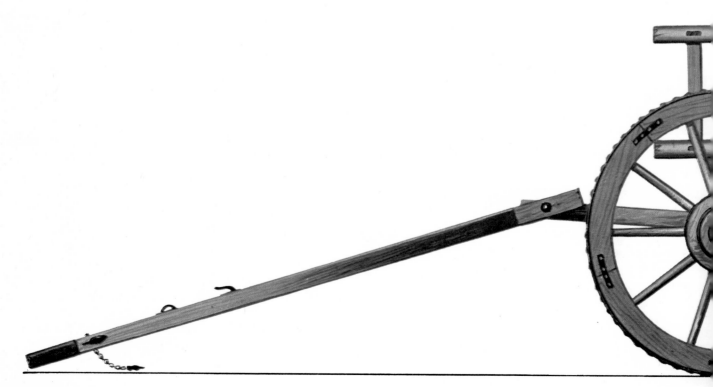

Standard British Guns in Service in 1776

Bronze Guns

Name	Calibre inches	Length feet	inches	Weight cwts	Range yards	Other names
3-pounder	2.91	3	0	1½	1200	Light Infantry 3-pdr
3-pounder	2.91	3	6	2½	1200	Light 3-pounder
6-pounder	3.668	4	6	5	1400	
6-pounder	3.668	5	0	5½	1400	Light 6-pounder
6-pounder	3.668	6	0	8¾	1400	New Medium 6-pdr
6-pounder	3.668	8	0	19¼	1400	Heavy 6-pounder
12-pounder	4.58	5	0	12	1400	New light 12-pdr
12-pounder	4.58	5	0	8¾	1400	Light 12-pdr
12-pounder	4.58	6	6	18	1400	New Medium 12-pdr
12-pounder	4.58	6	6	21¾	1400	Old Medium 12-pdr
12-pounder	4.58	9	0	31½	1400	Heavy 12-pdr
18-pounder	5.29	5	9	18	2000	New Light Model
24-pounder	5.72	5	0	16¾	1700	Light 24-pdr
24-pounder	5.72	6	3	24	1700	New 24-pdr
24-pounder	5.72	8	0	41¾	1700	Medium 24-pdr
24-pounder	5.72	9	6	53	1700	Heavy 24-pdr
32-pounder	6.30	9	8	42	1900	
32-pounder	6.30	10	0	55	1900	
42-pounder	6.95	8	0	52	2100	
42-pounder	6.95	10	6	66	2100	

Iron Guns

Name	Calibre inches	Length feet	inches	Weight cwts	Range yards
3-pounder	2.90	4	6	7¼	1400
6-pounder	3.67	6	0	16½	1500
6-pounder	3.67	8	0	22	1500
9-pounder	4.20	7	0	23	1800
9-pounder	4.20	7	6	24½	1800
12-pounder	4.62	7	6	29¼	1800
12-pounder	4.62	8	6	31½	1800
12-pounder	4.62	9	0	32	1800
12-pounder	4.62	9	6	34	1800
18-pounder	5.29	9	0	40	2300
18-pounder	5.29	9	6	42	2300
24-pounder	5.82	9	0	47½	2400
24-pounder	5.82	9	6	49	2400
24-pounder	5.82	10	0	52	2400
32-pounder	6.41	9	6	55	2900
32-pounder	6.41	10	0	58	2900
42-pounder	6.95	9	6	65	3100
42-pounder	6.95	10	0	67	3100

British service howitzers

Metal	Calibre inches	Length feet	inches	Weight cwts	Shell weight lbs	Range yards	
Bronze	4.4	1	10	3	8½	900	
Bronze	5½	2	9	10	16	1750	
Iron	5½	3	10	15	16	1800	
Bronze	4.58	3	9	6½	11	1200	12-pounder
Bronze	5.72	4	8½	13	21¼	1200	12-pounder
Bronze	6.30	5	3	18	28	1400	32-pounder
Bronze	8.0	3	1	12¾	46	1700	
Iron	8.0	4	0	22	46	1700	
Bronze	10.0	4	0	25¾	92	2000	
Iron	10.0	5	0	42	92	2000	

Mortars

Metal	Calibre inches	Service	Weight cwts	Shell weight lbs	Range yards
Bronze	8.0	Land	4¼	46	1600
Iron	8.0	Land	8	46	1700
Bronze	10.0	Land	10¼	93	1200
Bronze	10.0	Sea	33	93	3800
Iron	10.0	Land	16	93	2500
Iron	10.0	Sea	41	93	3800
Bronze	13.0	Land	25	200	1300
Bronze	13.0	Sea	82	200	4000
Iron	13.0	Land	36	200	2700
Iron	13.0	Sea	82¼	200	4000

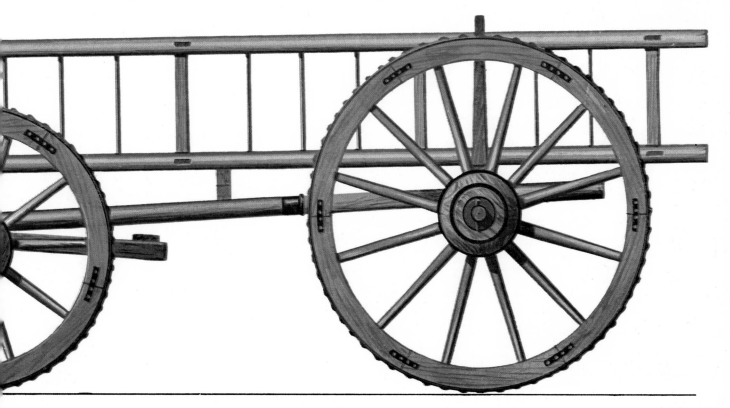

Below: British Lt. Col. Henry Hamilton (the 'Hair Buyer') surrendering Fort Sackville, at Vincennes, Indiana to George Rogers Clark in February 1779.

came, many of the members of these companies espoused the Revolutionary cause and took their expertise and sometimes some of their guns with them. Prominent among these men was Henry Knox, a volunteer artillerist of outstanding ability, who was instructed to take charge of the infant American artillery and organize it into a serviceable force. Knox was probably fortunate in having a smaller force to deal with than did Washington and von Steuben in their efforts to organize the infantry, but even allowing for that, Knox did a magnificent job and produced an artillery arm which was probably the most effective branch of the Continental Army.

The first units to be formed were independent companies from the various colonies: Lamb's New York Artillery Company, the Rhode Island Train of Artillery and so forth. But Knox was wide awake to the evils of colony-oriented units and in mid-1776 he re-organized the guns into four regiments of Continental Artillery. Originally, the establishment called for three regiments each of twelve companies and one of eight, but this was later changed to a standard ten-company regimental organization. The company varied in strength, depending upon what calibre of gun it possessed and how many of them, the usual gun strength being six to ten guns or howitzers per company.

The guns were a varied collection which might well have daunted a lesser man than Knox. Not for him the standardized issue of a Board of Ordnance; he was lucky to get anything, and thankful for small mercies. In the beginning the ordnance comprised whatever could be culled from various stations in the Colonies before the British Army came along and removed them to safekeeping. Ancient cannon on ramparts in long-neglected coast batteries were spirited away, guns of volunteer companies sequestered, ships cannon requisitioned. Stocks of powder and shot were acquired, while carpenters and wheelwrights set to work to produce field carriages in place of the ship and garrison carriages. The assembled collection ran from three-pounder to 24-pounder guns, with the larger calibres predominating. As a result of this imbalance, and because it was inevitable that this small stock of ordnance would be insufficient, gunfounding was begun in various places. The first to be produced were small one- and two-pounder swivel guns for naval use, but once the techniques had been mastered larger weapons were made. In 1776 some sixty 12-pounders and 18-pounders were cast in Pennsylvania, and shortly afterwards a standardized four-pounder light field gun was put into production.

Again, Henry Knox stepped in and brought order; instead of having cannon of all sorts and dimensions cast all over the place, he pressed for the concentration of manufacturing effort in one place, where it could be controlled and supervised, and where supply would be simplified, and he selected Springfield, Mass., as the gunmaking centre. In many respects this was a sensible move, but it also carried the elements of a gamble; had the British attacked and captured Springfield the ordnance supply arrangements would have collapsed into anarchy, but Knox was confident that the British commanders would neither appreciate the significance of Springfield nor, if they did, be capable of carrying out an operation against the town.

The supply situation was further eased in 1778 with the French alliance, when supplies of French cannon, shot and powder began to reach the Continental Army. The French artillery equipment was in the process of being radically revised by Gribeauval, and while little of his designs of equipment left France, his ideas on organization were assimilated by Knox, thereby beginning that unfortunate infatuation with French systems and equipment which bedevilled the American artillery for the next 150 years. That aside, the influx of excellent weapons was a welcome addition to the artillery strength.

The organization of the artillery followed the patterns set in Europe in that except for the light infantry-accompanying guns, the establishment was entirely fluid and determined by the requirements of a particular campaign. The 'Batallion Guns' which

were more or less permanently attached to the infantry, were based on an idea of Frederick the Great, though instead of being hand-drawn they were modified into horse-drawn 'galloper guns', three- and four-pounders drawn by two horses in tandem. These Galloper Guns were among the first attempts to give some degree of mobility to what had been, for centuries, a relatively static arm. Marshal Saxe once said that it was 'unlikely that the artillery will ever move any faster and impossible for it to move any slower', and only in the last four years of the 18th century were steps being taken to shake off this unfortunate image. But the improvement was more apparent than real; the Galloper Gun has a nice dashing sound to it and evokes images of a lightning descent onto the battlefield, a crashing volley of decisive effect, and a rapid gallop off to some other threatened point. The reality was somewhat different, since although the gun was rapidly portable, the ammunition followed along behind in a farm cart and the gunners trudged along on foot.

An interesting American Artillery deviant was the construction of two 'Floating Batteries' on the Charles River. These were flat-bottomed barges with superstructures of heavy timber. A 12- or 18-pounder (accounts are conflicting) was fitted at bow and stern, firing through embrasures which could be closed by wooden doors. A three-pounder was mounted at each side of the stern, and four 1½-pounder swivel guns were mounted on top of the superstructure. Musketry ports were cut in the sides, while propulsion was by a bank of oars on each side. These two craft were used to bombard British positions in Boston in September and October 1775, but their effect was negligible. With the British abandonment of Boston in the following year the floating batteries became redundant and were dismantled. Similar batteries were also built in Pennsylvania and used in various actions along the line of the Delaware River, but the practice was never widespread, since the peculiar conditions suited to the use of floating batteries occurred but rarely.

The field guns were of all sizes from eight-pounder to 24-pounder, usually of bronze, together with a handful of British 5½-inch and 8-inch howitzers, also bronze. As well as British guns of the various kinds already tabulated, the Continental Artillery was

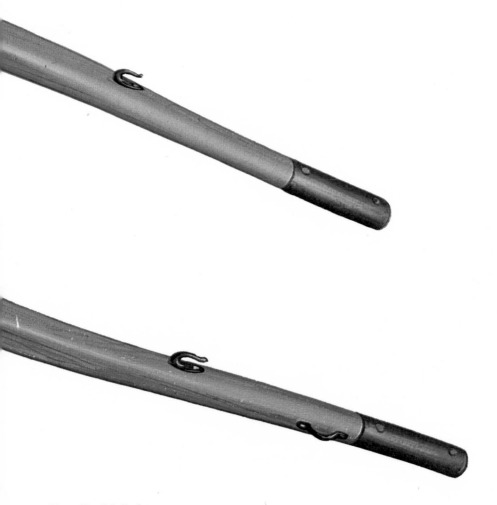

Above: English limber.

augmented by French guns, and the first of these was a batch shipped from France in 1777. Among this shipment was a collection of 31 Swedish four-pounders, lately used by France, excellent light guns and very acceptable. Less acceptable were the guns of French manufacture in the same shipment.

The French artillery at the commencement of the 18th century was in a sorry state; there was an even greater diversity of calibres and designs than in the British service, due mainly to the decentralization of control to the various Departments of France, whereby the local artillery commander could order guns cast to his own specification. Eventually, in 1732, the artillery was placed under the charge of General Vallière, with instructions to bring some sort of order into the service. This he did by ruthlessly discarding innumerable designs and standardizing on a range of calibres: 4-, 8-, 12-, 16- and 24-pounder guns, 8-inch and 12-inch mortars, and a 16-inch 'stone mortar'. The length and constructional details were laid down in some detail, as were even the engraving and decorations to be allowed on the guns. Thus the four-pounder had the cascable engraved with a stylized face in a sunburst, while the 16-pounder cascable was cast into the form of a Medusa head.

Unfortunately, while Vallière attended to the ordnance in great detail, he was entirely careless about how the ordnance was mounted, and the carriages beneath his guns were of every size and shape imaginable, their only common factor being their relative clumsiness. His other mistake lay in the proportions of the guns. His 12-pounder, for example, weighed $31\frac{1}{2}$ hundredweights for a length of eight feet ten inches. This was very close to the old pattern of British Heavy twelve-pounder which was virtually obsolescent and had been replaced by guns of less than one ton in weight. All Vallière's guns were the same in this respect; they were too heavy and too long, being based on out-of-date theories, and they were all inferior to guns of similar calibres in other countries. It was for this reason that Henry Knox was

disappointed when he received the first shipment of Vallière guns. He was particularly bitter about the French four-pounders; these weighed $11\frac{1}{2}$ hundredweight, and Knox considered they each carried sufficient surplus metal to allow them to be melted down and recast, two four-pounders providing enough bronze to make five light six-pounders. It is said that as well as directing his own gunfounders to set about doing this he also submitted his views to the French, but they refused. They were, in fact, on the point of a completely fresh reorganization under the guidance of Gribeauval, an exceptionally astute artilleryman, and while they were quite willing to assist the United States by giving them their redundant cannon, they had far too involved a program on their hands to be inclined to go to any degree of trouble for outsiders.

Gribeauval's system embraced every item of artillery store: guns, howitzers, mortars, their carriages and limbers, ammunition carts, even bridging equipment, and it gains a mention here because it was the system eventually adopted by the United States artillery after the war; it also seems likely that a small number of Griebeauval cannon reached America in time to be employed by French troops de Grasse landed at Yorktown.

The basis of his system was the rigid division of ordnance into field and siege natures, everything above twelve-pounder being classed as siege artillery. There was nothing particularly new in this, since a similar split had formed the basis of Gustavus Adolphus' reorganization of the Swedish Artillery in the early part of the 17th century, but Gribeauval went much farther, redesigning weapons so as to pare off excess weight and standardizing his guns at eighteen calibres length with a weight of fifty times the weight of their solid shot. Under this system his twelve-pounder had a length of six feet eleven inches and weight of $5\frac{1}{2}$ hundredweights, an extremely light and slender gun and a great improvement over any contemporary designs. One of the most notable and easily recognizable features of Gribeauval's carriages was the provision of two sets of trunnion housings, one in the usual place over the axletree and one set back along the trail about one-third of the distance from the axletree to the trail end. This allowed the piece to be shifted back from the firing position in the front trunnion mountings to a travelling position in the rear mountings, which gave better balance and stability while on the move, spreading the load more evenly between the wheels of the gun carriage and the wheels of the limber. It was a feature widely copied in the remaining years of the muzzle-loading era, and indeed the principle remains today, since many modern pieces of artillery have the barrel retracted along the trail to improve the travelling characteristics, although without actually transferring the trunnions to a fresh location.

The locally-manufactured American guns were largely copies of British standard models, since these were the easiest to obtain for the preparation of patterns. A few were constructed on the lines advocated by John Muller, who was the Professor of Artillery and Fortification at the Royal Academy, Woolwich. His book *A Treatise of Artillery* had been published in 1756 and was the standard text of the day, and a pirate copy was published in Philadelphia in 1779 which became the handbook of the American artillerymen. In this book Muller had published plans of cannon based on sundry theories of his own, and as a result the few cannon which were ever built to Muller's ideas were made in America. Despite his official position, his theories were never accepted in Britain.

Top: Storming the British positions at Yorktown.
Above: English traveling forge (left) and American powder cart (right).

Ammunition

The variety of ammunition available in 1775 was far from being the wide-ranging armory of modern times, but on the other hand it was not restricted to solid ball. Fortunately for all concerned, young Henry Shrapnel had not yet had his inspiration and the shrapnel shell was still thirty years away——it was not until the War of 1812 that the Americans were to experience the 'tarnation English split-shot'——but even in default of that particular missile there were sufficient varieties to make life dangerous.

For the muskets and pistols, of course, the standard projectile was the common lead ball, though even there there is a certain amount of evidence to suggest that the American farmers introduced one of their hunting variations into warfare, paving the way for the military acceptance in the later United States Army of the 'Buck and Ball' loading. The Massachusetts Provincial Congress, in 1779, when listing the accoutrements to be provided by recruits, included 'a hundred buckshot' as well as 'forty leaden balls

fitted to your gun'. Buck and ball loading meant that the full calibre ball was supplemented by a few smaller balls of buckshot so as to form a combination of precision and scatter projectiles. As we have seen the standard musket was not quite as accurate as tradition and folklore would have us believe, and a charge of buck and ball offered the chance of wounding, if not killing, with the buckshot component if the full calibre ball should miss. A similar hope lay behind the contemporary fashion for loading two balls over a reduced powder charge. The charge had to be reduced because the greater weight of the double loading meant greater inertia to be overcome and hence lower velocity. A normal cartridge exploded behind this extra mass would be likely to damage the barrel, expand the chamber or in extreme cases blow the breach plug out of the musket. This, at any rate, was the ballistic theory of the matter, but few private soldiers of those days (or officers either) had the remotest conception of

Below: A collection of proof marks used by the armies of the American Revolutionary War.

English weapons markings
1. London proofmarks, 1637, usually on the barrel.
2. London proofmarks, 1672.
3. London proofmarks, 1702. The 'V' stamp denotes the first rough proofing 'viewing'; GP gunmakers proof was the final proof. This applies to proofmarks 1–3.
4. Barrel proofs, Royal Armory.
5. Typical private proofmarks——Birmingham before 1813.
6. Birmingham proofmarks, 1813.
7. Private proofmarks, Board of Ordnance, struck twice on a barrel, at the Tower of London for a fee.
8. Foreigners proofmark on London Gunmakers for non-members, used with two regular proofs 1 and 3 above, after 1741.
9. Viewers, inspectors mark for government arms; the numeral indicates the inspector.
10. Ordnance Storekeeper's proofmark, used on the side of the butt after 1770; retroactive to earlier weapons.
11. Board of Ordnance ownership mark, mostly on stock, replaced by WD (War Department), 1855.
12. Government ownership stamp on lock plates.
13. Royal cipher for Georgius Rex (Georges I–III), used under a crown on lock plates and on sword blades.
14. Royal cipher during Queen Anne's reign, 1702–1714.
15. East India Company mark, used on stock or barrel.

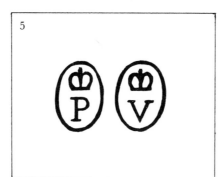

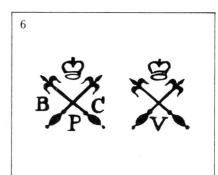

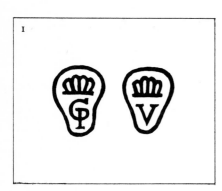

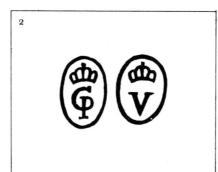

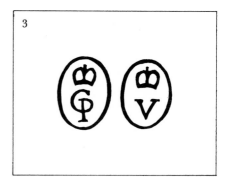

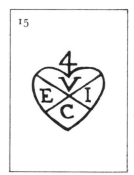

French weapons markings
16. Lock markings 'AR' for Inspector Desjardins, 1718–1755; MBE for Royal Factory at Maubeuge.
17. Charleville mark.
18. 'SE' for Saint-Etienne Factory.
19. 1728 barrel marking.
20. 1728 barrel marking.
21. '67' denotes the last two digits of the year of manufacture, 1767.
22. Controllers' mark on lock and barrel; B is his initial.

Other European weapons markings
23. Liège, Belgium, 1672–1810.
24. Liège, Belgium, 1810.
25. Amsterdam control mark on barrels.
26. Denmark (including Norway), 1746–1766.
27. Hen for Henneberg in the Holy Roman Empire (the Germanies); SVL for the town of Suhl.
28. Typical Spanish barrel marking.
29. Mark, originally Passau and Solingen in the Holy Roman Empire, later copied throughout Europe on swordblades.
30. Shotley Bridge on English swordblades.

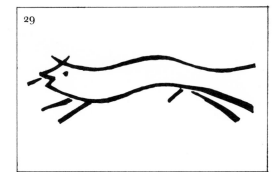

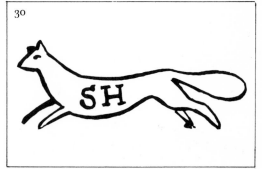

ballistic theory; fortunately for them the factor of safety built into the weapons of the day was generally sufficient to withstand the occasional overload.

With artillery the range of possible projectiles was rather more diverse. The standard was, of course, the simple cast-iron spherical shot or cannonball, which was useful against both men and material. But its effect against either was solely kinetic, the smashing powder derived from its mass and velocity. And the greater the range, the less this became, so that at extreme ranges when the velocity had fallen and the ball struck the ground, it would roll and bounce sufficiently slowly to permit an agile man to leap clear of its path.

The prospect of utilizing the explosive force of

English sling cart (*above*) and sling wagon (*below*).

gunpowder in a hollow projectile had attracted artillerymen for many years. The first recorded attempt at using shells dates from 1588, but there were a lot of drawbacks. The earliest attempts relied on the friction generated between the gunpowder and the roughcast interior of the shell. When the missile struck the ground, the powder inside would be thrown about violently and as it grated over the metal there would be sufficient friction to generate heat and thus ignite and explode the powder. True enough, it did——sometimes. Unfortunately there was more or less the same agitation and friction when the shell was fired from the gun, as the sudden acceleration up the bore caused the loose powder to be flung about, which was likely to produce premature

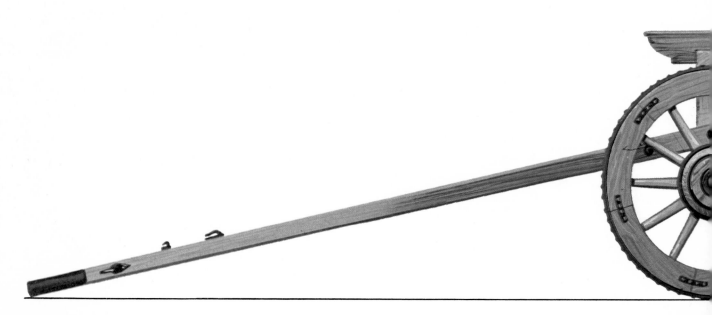

ignition of the charge while the shell was still inside the gun.

A somewhat safer system was to put the powder inside a cloth bag inside the shell, filling it tightly so that little or no movement could take place. Ignition could then be done by a length of slowmatch ——twine soaked in saltpetre and spirits of wine—— pushed into a hole on the shell and retained by a clay plug. The only problem now lay in lighting this primitive fuse, and the first system adopted was never exactly popular with the gunners, for reasons which will be obvious; after the gun had been loaded with its powder charge, the shell was loaded with its fuse towards the muzzle. The gunner then thrust his portfire or match down the barrel of the gun and lit the shell fuse; he then smartly pulled the portfire out and applied it to the touch hole to fire the gun. It all sounds very simple, and doubtless the man who thought of it was of the same opinion, but there was a grave danger that during the loading of the charge a trickle of gunpowder might have been deposited in the bore, and the smouldering portfire could easily ignite this while the gunner was groping around trying to make contact with the shell fuse. Result: sudden discharge of the gun and, at best, an amputated arm.

An equally hare-brained idea was to provide two gunners with portfires, one to light the shell and one to fire the cannon; there are so many possibilities for disaster in this combination that the mind reels. But these perilous games were discarded when it was realized that the discharge of the cannon was sufficient to ignite the fuse without any special arrangements being necessary. At first the shell was loaded so that the fuse was alongside the powder, and the explosion of the charge lit the fuse. Unfortunately this frequently failed, due to the blast of the explosion blowing the fuse out immediately after lighting it; sometimes in extreme cases the explosion would collapse the clay plug and explode the shell in the gun. A better way was to load the shell with the fuse towards the muzzle and the wash of flame over the shell due to the windage would ignite the fuse quite satisfactorily.

For all this improvement, the shell was still a capricious beast, and the average gunner was more inclined to rely on solid shot. But even the most reactionary could hardly deny the advantage of an explosive filling when it came to a question of demolishing a building or spreading fragments over a wide area in order to inflict casualties. Gradually the shell gained acceptance, and as the fuse was improved so the reliability improved with it. Instead of the original length of slowmatch, a wooden peg carrying a thin filling of powder was developed. The peg tapered so that it could be driven into the fuse hole of the shell, and the exterior surface was marked off in divisions. After the gunner had assessed the range to the target

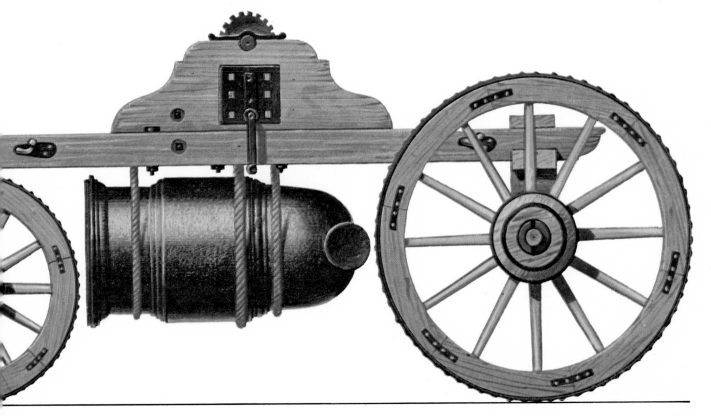

he took a knife and cut off the fuse to such a length that the train of powder within would just burn through as the shell reached the ground at the end of its flight. At the top of the peg was a recess filled with a paste of fine powder and spirits of wine, covered with a tar-plaster. With the fuse cut to length, the gunner removed the closing plug from the shell, filled it with gunpowder, and then drove the fuse tightly home with a mallet. After loading the gun with the powder charge, he ripped away the plaster to expose the primed fuse head and loaded the shell. On firing the flash ignited the priming, and this in turn ignited the central filling of powder. Since the lower end of the fuse had been cut off, exposing the powder channel, once the flame reached the end it would flash across to the shell filling and that was that.

There were other attempts to enlarge the effective zone of the projectile without, however, introducing the hazards of gunpowder or the uncertainty of fuses into the proceedings. In a manner analogous to the buck and ball loads used with muskets, some multiple loadings were used with cannon. Again, it was not new; early in the 15th century 'Langridge'——loose metal and stones——had been loaded over a wad to give a shotgun effect, and over the intervening years this idea had been codified into two basic groups of scatter projectiles, case shot and grape shot.

Case was a direct descendant of langridge; as the name implied, it consisted of a case of light metal packed with a large number of musket balls. When fired the case collapsed under the shock of the explosion and its remains, together with the musket balls, were ejected from the muzzle in an expanding cone which was highly lethal out to a range of two or three hundred yards. For longer ranges, missiles with better 'carrying power' were needed, and this led to grape shot. In this the container was simply a canvas bag and the contents a number of lead or iron balls an inch or more in diameter. In order to turn this bag of balls into something more convenient to handle and easier to load, a light cord was lashed around in order to pull the bundle into a more or

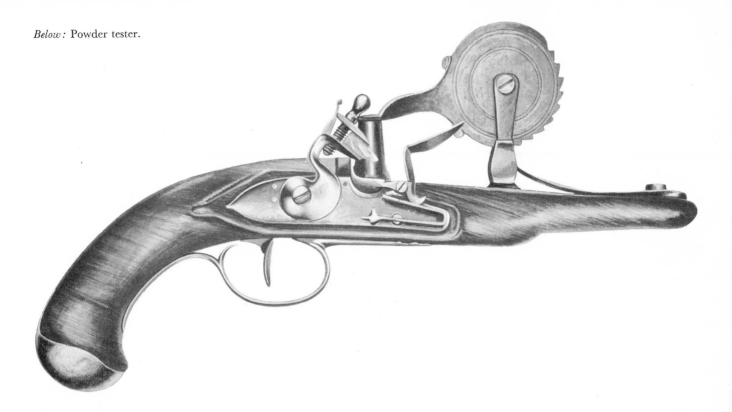

less cylindrical shape. The resulting appearance, reminiscent of a bunch of grapes, led to the 'grape-shot' title.

Grape and case between them could blanket the area from the gun's muzzle to about 600 yards distance, a sufficient coverage to deal with infantry or cavalry charges. Beyond that a massed body of troops was relatively safe from the scatter projectiles, and a single ball was unlikely to have effect on more than one or two men. In order to save using shells, some odd types of projectile were tried in the hopes of reaping a better harvest. Split shot, for example; although in 1812 the Americans called British shrapnel 'split-shot', this was due to their initial ignorance of its design and operation, and split shot proper was simply two solid half-balls bound together with twine so that they could be loaded as one unit but would fly apart after leaving the gun muzzle and take divergent paths, highly unpredictable due to their asymmetrical shape. They were relatively uncommon. A more effective missile was chain shot, either two split shot connected by a short length of chain or two whole shot similarly connected. On leaving the muzzle the shot would separate until the restraining chain prevented further movement, after which the missile would swing and scythe through the air——and through anything else which impeded its progress. Chain shot was particularly popular with naval gunners, since it was well adapted for carrying away masts and rigging, but they were not entirely

unknown in land warfare, where their effect on a mass of troops, foot or mounted, was devastating. Of similar effect, and easier to manufacture, was bar shot; two shot or two cylinders of iron of the correct calibre, joined by an iron bar a foot or eighteen inches long.

Another predominantly naval projectile which found some application on land was red hot shot. This was reputedly invented by Stefan Batory, King of Poland, during the 16th century, and its efficiency as a fire-raiser against tar-steeped wooden ships led to its universal adoption as an anti-ship projectile. But on land it still had its uses, notably against defensive works; while of little value against European-style masonry fortifications, it was formidable against the wooden structures within a defensive line and against rudimentary fieldworks of logs. It was also widely used by coast defense batteries, and an American battery at Yorktown sank a British warship by a well-placed red hot shot.

Fortunately the performance involved in firing red hot shot was cumbersome——suited to protracted siege operations but rarely capable of being brought into use in the more fluid actions of open warfare. The prime requirement was, of course, a forge to heat the shot. This was an awkward piece of ironmongery to haul about on the battlefield, and it demanded a supply of fuel as well as a squad of men to tend it, operate the bellows and bring the shot to red heat. Once this was done the gun was loaded with the usual

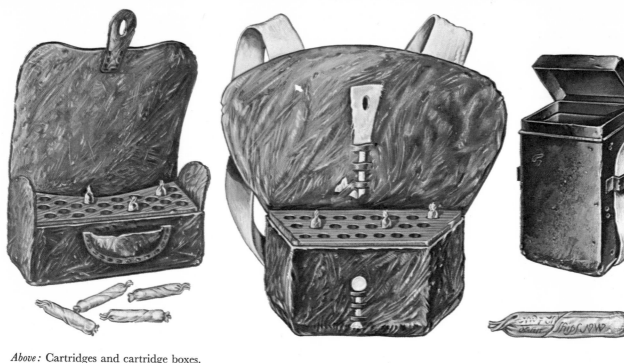

Above: Cartridges and cartridge boxes.

(*Left*) Waist cartridge box. Worn by special troops, e.g. Light Infantry and Cavalry. Constructed of black calf leather, smaller than the shoulder box and worn at the front, it was attached to the waist belt by means of two loops on the back of the box. A pocket was sewn on to the front to carry extra flints.

(*Centre*) Shoulder cartridge box. Made from black calf leather with a protecting flap. Inside a hardwood block drilled with 20 to 30 holes, held and secured the paper cartridges. The block was removable to allow a dozen new flints to be stored in the bottom of the box. Hung by a linen or leather strap on the right and slightly to the rear of the soldier to allow easy access but avoiding the next man in rank.

(*Right*) Tin canister. The shortage of waterproof cartridge boxes gave birth to this excellent substitute. It could carry 36 cartridges in layers of four. It had the advantages of being light, fire and waterproof. It was hinged at the rear and would fall shut after the cartridge was removed, thus preventing accidental ignition of the remaining cartridges. The tin was japanned to prevent rusting and had tin loops on either side plus one underneath, taking a $1\frac{1}{2}''$ strap.

(*Bottom right*) The cartridge. The preparation of cartridges was an important camp duty. During battle the loading of a musket from a powder horn was a risky undertaking. A ready manufactured tube of powder and ball was an obvious advantage. The process was: paper rolled around a former— a six-inch dowell hollowed out at one end to take the ball. A piece of twine enclosing the paper tube below the ball. Black powder for the charge was inserted and the top twisted to secure the charge. A small amount of powder to prime the pan was added. The cartridge was made slightly narrower than the bore, because the barrel became fouled with burned powder from previous discharges.

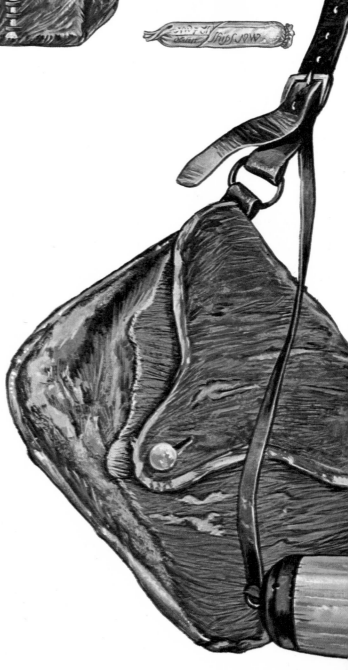

Below: Hunting bags. Hunting, game or rifle bags were generally made from hides or leathers and accommodated lead balls, extra flints, priming or powder horns, patch boards, tomahawks, rifle knives and hunting, fighting or scalping knives.

149

powder charge, and a tight-fitting dry wooden wad rammed on top. This was followed by a wet wad of rags and oakum well-soaked in water, intended to insulate the powder from the shot during the brief time the two would be together in the gun. The shot was then brought quickly from the forge, loaded and rammed, and the gun fired.

Although this sounds a hazardous proposition, the records tend to show that the accident rate with red hot shot was no greater than with any other form of projectile. This probably reflects the likelihood that the gunners, well aware of what was at stake, took a little more care than usual when operating with it.

The weapons of the American Revolutionary War exhibited all the variety and style that the 18th century could muster. Most types of artillery, edged weapons and small arms which existed durign the period were used, and their manufacture, though primarily British, ranged from indigenous American arms to those of French and other Continental origin. But the use of these weapons was advanced during the war, and despite the fact that the Revolutionary War was revolutionary largely in political terms and not in military usage, the development of the Brown Bess and the Kentucky Rifle cannot be ignored in the context of weapons development during the 18th century. It was in the employment of these weapons that subtle, though nevertheless important changes were apparent. This was the first time in modern history that a major land army was fully supplied by sea over a distance of some 3000 miles. Despite the fact that the French and Spanish navies did what they could to sever these supply lines, they were maintained throughout the war notwithstanding all the red tape and bureaucratic complications which such an enterprise entailed. But in the field, the American armies facing the well-supplied British were, initially, and for some units consistently, irregular forces. They were badly and seldom paid. They were, on the whole, clothed and provisioned in a haphazard way. The Battle of Yorktown was a classic siege fought in a classic manner. Since it was the decisive battle of the war, it tends to obscure the fact that most of the war was fought by irregular troops against a regular army. This was certianly true in the case of Francis Marion and George Rogers Clark; less true in the case of Washington and Arnold, when he fought for the United States; not at all true for the French under Rochambeau. But it was largely an irregular army which defeated the British regulars in the field. The myth was cracked; an irregular force could win against trained troops if support of the regulars by the home country were something less than wholehearted. It was a lesson which was brought home to European strategists on the rolling hills near Valmy in 1792. The point was made more forcefully by Napoleon in the Italian campaign of 1796–7 and again during his many victorious expeditions against the Russians, Prussians and Austrians a decade later. The debate is far from over. The revolutionary style of warfare inaugurated by the American War of Independence has often been employed in recent decades, from Yugoslavia to Algeria to Vietnam. In this sense the Armies of the American Revolution made a lasting contribution to revolutionary warfare.

The American Revolutionary War created heroes and villains, scapegoats and martyrs. From Washington and Lafayette to Cornwallis and Benedict Arnold,

Opposite: Two powder horns. The etched maps helped their
owner to find his way home.
Below: English, French and American plug and socket
bayonets (from left to right: English plug, English socket,
French plug, French socket, American plug and American
socket).

Flint knapping

An arm or lump is broken off the excavated flint after being warmed to reduce moisture, a process called quartering. Next the lump is placed on a block and 'flaked' into long strips—— the longer the better. By turning the lump with the hand and working round the outer edge, the knapper can produce many flints from one piece. Taking each flake the craftsman flint knapper shapes the flint for its striking edge, which must be sharp and truly square. The next stage is concerned with cutting the individual flints. By holding the flake over the edge of a steel block to the width of a flint, the knapper cuts off a flint with a sharp tap with the knapping hammer. Finally each flint is trimmed and cleaned before being suited into pistol and musket sizes and then packed in casks of 500 and 1000. A good knapper can produce 400 flints an hour——and still does at Brandon in Suffolk, England, where the interest in muzzle loading shooting has increased over the past twenty years.

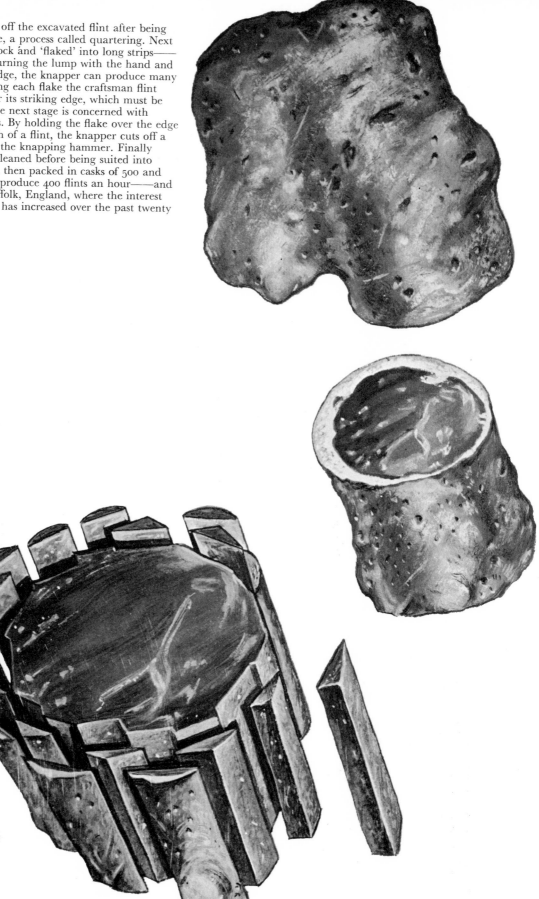

the tragedy of the collapse of the British Empire in
the 18th century is matched by the triumph of the
American Republic. The men at the top made the
great decisions. In fact, if King George III and his
Prime Minister, Lord North, had got it right, there
might have been no war at all. But once the decision
not to compromise with the rebels was taken in 1775,
and war became inevitable, the way the war was
fought and won or lost depended not so much on
decisions in London or Paris——indeed, not even by
decisions in Washington's or Burgoyne's camps——
but by decisions reached on the field of battle. In any
war it is the men in the field and the weapons which
they use——and how they use them——which brings
the ultimate victory or defeat. This book has shown
that there was no great superiority of weapons on
either side. Many of the weapons, artillery pieces,
pistols, muskets, swords and rifles were similar and
in some cases identical to both sides. In the final
analysis victory for the Americans came down to two
things. First, they were fighting for a cause in which
they believed, while the British fought because it was
their job to do so. As British public opinion gradually
shifted to indifference or even hostility to their
government's policy, the longer the war continued
the better the poorly trained Americans' chances were
against the large and highly qualified professional
British armies. Second, the effect of French and other
allied assistance to the Americans' cause cannot be
overemphasized. The French and Dutch provided
money and arms for the Americans. They and the
Spanish provided valuable naval assistance to the
war, which proved so vital to the result of the Battle
of Yorktown. And the French provided seasoned
commanders and men who knew their business——
the business of war. To them——and to Washington
——all credit must be given. But, as in all wars,
without the support and increasing expertise of the
men who actually fought the battles, the Revolution
could never have been won. For ultimately it is the
men and their weapons which decide a war every
time.

By the KING.

A PROCLAMATION,

Declaring the Cessation of Arms, as well by Sea as Land, agreed upon between His Majesty, the Most Christian King, the King of *Spain*, the States General of the *United Provinces*, and the United States of *America*, and enjoining the Observance thereof.

GEORGE R.

HEREAS Provisional Articles were signed at *Paris*, on the Thirtieth Day of *November* last, between Our Commissioner for treating of Peace with the Commissioners of the United States of *America* and the Commissioners of the said States, to be inserted in and to constitute the Treaty of Peace proposed to be concluded between Us and the said United States, when Terms of Peace should be agreed upon between Us and His Most Christian Majesty: And whereas Preliminaries for restoring Peace between Us and His Most Christian Majesty were signed at *Versailles* on the Twentieth Day of *January* last, by the Ministers of Us and the Most Christian King: And whereas Preliminaries for restoring Peace between Us and the King of *Spain* were also signed at *Versailles* on the Twentieth Day of *January* last, between the Ministers of Us and the King of *Spain*: And whereas, for putting an End to the Calamity of War as soon and as far as may be possible, it hath been agreed between Us, His Most Christian Majesty, the King of *Spain*, the States General of the *United Provinces*, and the United States of *America*, as follows; that is to say,

That such Vessels and Effects as should be taken in the *Channel* and in the *North Seas*, after the Space of Twelve Days, to be computed from the Ratification of the said Preliminary Articles, should be restored on all Sides; That the Term should be One Month from the *Channel* and the *North Seas* as far as the *Canary Islands* inclusively, whether in the Ocean or in the *Mediterranean*; Two Months from the said *Canary Islands* as far as the Equinoctial Line or Equator; and lastly, Five Months in all other Parts of the World, without any Exception, or any other more particular Description of Time or Place.

And whereas the Ratifications of the said Preliminary Articles between Us and the Most Christian King, in due Form, were exchanged by the Ministers of Us and of the Most Christian King, on the Third Day of this instant *February*; and the Ratifications of the said Preliminary Articles between Us and the King of *Spain* were exchanged between the Ministers of Us and of the King of *Spain*, on the Ninth Day of this instant *February*; from which Days respectively the several Terms above-mentioned, of Twelve Days, of One Month, of Two Months, and of Five Months, are to be computed: And whereas it is Our Royal Will and Pleasure that the Cessation of Hostilities between Us and the States General of the *United Provinces*, and the United States of *America*, should be agreeable to the Epochs fixed between Us and the Most Christian King:

We have thought fit, by and with the Advice of Our Privy Council, to notify the same to all Our loving Subjects; and We do declare, that Our Royal Will and Pleasure is, and We do hereby strictly charge and command all Our Officers, both at Sea and Land, and all other Our Subjects whatsoever, to forbear all Acts of Hostility, either by Sea or Land, against His Most Christian Majesty, the King of *Spain*, the States General of the *United Provinces*, and the United States of *America*, their Vassals or Subjects, from and after the respective Times above-mentioned, and under the Penalty of incurring Our highest Displeasure.

Given at Our Court at *Saint James's*, the Fourteenth Day of *February*, in the Twenty-third Year of Our Reign, and in the Year of Our Lord One thousand seven hundred and eighty-three.

God save the King.

LONDON:

Printed by CHARLES EYRE and WILLIAM STRAHAN, Printers to the King's most Excellent Majesty. 1783.

Acknowledgements

The editor would like to thank David Eldred, graduate of the Royal College of Art, and now a free-lance designer of books for Weidenfeld and Nicolson, Octopus Books and *The Economist* newspaper, for his assistance in designing this book. The editor would also like to thank Judith Harkison for her help in collecting some of the illustrations used in this book.

Picture Credits

North Sea

CARRICKFERGUS ★

★ **DOGGER BANK**

★ **FLAMBOROUGH HEA**

Atlantic Ocean

Den Helder
Amsterdam
London
Chatham
Plymouth
Portsmouth
Boulogne
NETHERLANDS
AUSTRIAN
NETHERLANDS
Brussels

USHANT ★ Brest

Paris

Quiberon Bay

H

FRANCE

Toulon

Lisbon
Madrid

MINORCA

Cadiz
GIBRALTAR ★

Mediterranean S.